M000078426

TOMORROW, WE RIDE...

TOMORROW, WE RIDE…

Jean Bobet

Translated from the French
by Adam Berry

TOMORROW, WE RIDE…

English edition first published in 2008
by:

Mousehold Press   Sport and Publicity
Victoria Cottage   75 Fitzjohns Avenue
Constitution Opening   and   Hampstead
Norwich NR3 4BD   London, NW3 6PD
www.mousehold-press.co.uk   www.sport&publicity.co.uk

Reprinted 2009
Reprinted 2010

Originally published in France by La Table Ronde,
under the title *Demain, on roule…*

The English edition of this book has been made possible with
financial support from the Centre National du Livre

Text copyright ©Jean Bobet, 2004
Translation copyright ©Adam Berry, 2008

All rights reserved. No part of this publication may be
reproduced, stored in a retrieval system, or transmitted, in any
form or by any means, electronic, mechanical, photocopying,
recording, or otherwise, without the prior consent of the publisher.

ISBN 978 1 874739 51 7

CONTENTS

Publishers' Note

This is the second translation of a European cycling book we have published. The first, *Induráin: a tempered passion*, was an outstanding biography written by a prize-winning author and journalist who was a serious fan of the Spanish champion. This present book was written by an equally distinguished cycling journalist, but there the similarity ends. Jean Bobet was not a mere fan of a legendary cycling champion, but the brother of one, and an excellent rider in his own right. Louison Bobet, World Champion, multiple Classics winner, and the first man to win the Tour de France three years in succession, was a massive superstar of his time. Although not endowed with quite the same natural ability as his friend, the great Italian Fausto Coppi, he was tough and courageous and became renowned as a fighter, as well as being an innovator in new training methods. And alongside him rode younger brother Jean, often in the jersey of the French national team. Jean retired from racing in 1959, but continued to ride for pleasure with his older brother until Louison's tragically early death.

Tomorrow, we ride... is a fascinating story of two brothers – one a brilliant, internationally celebrated racing cyclist; the other more academically inclined, torn between his twin loves of literature and cycling. It skillfully evokes life in rural France during the post-war, reconstruction era, and the century-old place that bicycle racing occupies in French culture. That love affair with cycling and cycling people runs through the book. 'We always understood each other best on bikes,' he writes. 'We had always needed a bike beneath us.'

There is no doubt that but for his brother, and his own abiding affection for the bicycle, Jean's life would have been very different. As a young post-graduate student of literature at the University of Aberdeen, he received a brief, hand-written note from Louison, already a National Road-race Champion, urging him to return to France and re-cast his life as a professional cyclist. With his thesis ('The Hero in Hemingway') stalled, he abandoned a budding literary/academic career, and took to the roads of France.

There is a mild irony to this in that while Jean Bobet eventually came to be the author of several distinguished cycling books, Hemingway never got to write the novel about bike-racing that he often contemplated. 'French is the only language it [bike-racing] has ever been written in properly and the terms are all French and that is what makes it so hard,' he explained. And that, of course, is the difficulty faced by the English publishers of a cycling book originally written in French.

Nowadays, the internationalisation of professional cycling has rendered this difficulty less acute. *Le peloton* is 'the peloton' in any language; we all know what *bidons* and *musettes* are; we can distinguish between a *rouleur* and a *grimpeur*. Nevertheless, French cycling has produced a particularly rich argot of which Jean Bobet naturally makes ample use. Literal translation would render much of that vocabulary meaningless in English. With his approval, therefore, when we have not used a familiar French word we have tended towards a rather free translation which draws upon the colloquialisms of the English cycling fraternity which we believe conveys their essential meaning. We leave it to the reader to judge how successful we have been.

Richard Allchin, Adrian Bell, Mick Clark

Picture credits
Original prints on loan from the Roger St Pierre collection (1, 8, 10, 11, 13, 14; Courtesy Jean Bobet (2, 3, 5, 6, 7, 9, 15, 16, 17, 22); Miroir Archive/Photosport International (20, 21); Cycling Weekly (19); Courtesy The Horton Collection (12); Richard Allchin (4); Courtesy Tony Hewson (18).

Publishers' acknowledgements
We would like to express our gratitude to the following:
Adam Berry for his sensitive translation of the original; Alice Déon at La Table Ronde for her help and encouragement; Roger St Pierre both for his kind offer to provide us with a foreword to this edition and for giving us access to his photographic archive; Marilyn Bell for proofreading the manuscript; Keith Bingham, Brian Palmer, Phil Liggett, Luke Edwardes-Evans, David Harmon, The Bears, Dan Lloyd, Rocky, SC and Patti Esposito for their constant support. We would like also to give a special posthumous thanks to the late Chas Messenger.

Foreword

As a 12-year old toiling my way through grammar school, I was next to useless at French. Six out of 100 was my norm. But then I discovered Louison Bobet, and the Tour de France. My elder brother, David, had been on a youth hostelling tour in Normandy and brought me back some wonderful sepia-printed and picture-filled souvenir Tour mags covering Louison Bobet's glorious triumphs in the world's biggest, toughest bike race. And I was soon aware that there was another Bobet brother, a super-domestique who was at Louison's side in good times and bad, a man of intellect, who had studied at Aberdeen University and spoke good English but who chose to suffer on a bicycle alongside his brother rather than opt for a softer and probably more financially rewarding career as an academic. Jean, a studious and sensitive man, was the constant companion extraordinaire in Louison's career, his rock in a storm, and this book is his story. Reading it is like rediscovering all my yesterdays.

Jean, of course, was no slouch himself when it came to top class racing, winning the 1955 Paris–Nice after taking the first stage with a fine solo ride that put him 1'-18" ahead of the leading group. He held that precise advantage through to the end, after Louison had won the third stage – a unique result for the brothers. Jean achieved many other fine results in a racing career that was something to be proud of. Ironically, it might have been better still, had he not ridden almost invariably in the service of his more naturally talented older brother. On the other hand, he might not have started cycle racing in the first place but for Louison!

This highly entertaining and deeply informative book reminds me of what attracted me in the first place to those still wonderfully evocative Tour magazine photos of riders ripping punctured tyres off rims, grabbing at musettes and bidons in the feed station, scraping themselves off the tarmac after a fall, labouring their way up soaring Alpine passes or soaking in scum-filled bathtubs at stage end. All of those images made the captions oh-so-easy to understand, thereby making sense of a language that had so wilfully evaded me when presented as a mass of unfathomable words and complicated grammar scrawled on a classroom blackboard.

The bedroom walls of other British schoolboys in the 50s might have been given over to pictures of footballer Stanley Mathews or cricketer Len Hutton, but on mine was a glorious full-colour poster of Louison Bobet, majestically climbing the Izoard pass on his way to his first Tour success, in 1953. Two years on, he completed the hat-trick to become the first rider to win Le Tour three years in succession.

That extraordinarily evocative picture was soon joined by equally inspiring shots of the greats of what was surely the golden age of bicycle racing – Fausto Coppi, Hugo Koblet, Ferdi Kubler, Rik Van Steenbergen – but Bobet was always given pride of place, and in a number of those shots there was brother Jean right by his side. I retained a lasting affection for the Bobets, the talented baker's sons from Brittany. I even had my own bicycle re-sprayed orange and blue to mimic Louison's Tour-winning Stella machine.

As Jean recalls, his brother was the consummate all-rounder. Of bigger build than Coppi, he could, on his day, trade pedal strokes with purist climbers like Charly Gaul, the fabled 'Angel of the Mountains', and actually drop them – a treatment he imperiously meted out to the diminutive Luxembourger on the pitiless Mont Ventoux in 1955. A rather weak sprinter at the start of his career, Louison steadily improved his finishing powers to the point where, on a glorious spring day in 1956, he swept onto the Roubaix vélodrome to outpace the super-sprinters and add Paris–Roubaix to a glorious palmares that already included a world title and most of the other great one-day races.

In those days, I was Bobet, at least, that's who I imagined I was as I toiled over South Weald Hill on my training rides, fantasizing that pimple to be the upper slopes of the Galibier and re-casting the assorted first, second, third and junior category clubmen trying to outpace me to the top in the roles of Ockers, De Bruyne, Geminiani, Robic, Magni, Fornara, Schaer and Poblet and the other second-string heroes of my fertile imagination.

There was something else that marked Bobet out as my role model. Apart from his beautifully classy riding style, superb physique and attacking approach to racing, was his humanity. Here was a rider who had worked hard to get to the top, a man who had his moments of self-doubt and internal turmoil, but who fought back and triumphed, often against the odds. And he was a man who never forgot the debt he owed to his brother.

Wind the clock forward just over half a century. I had been in Brittany for a week, exploring the delights of this far-flung western province, its rich cultural heritage and wonderful food. I'd enjoyed invigorating thalassotherapy spa treatments and reminded myself that it was the Bobets who had established the first such seawater health treatment centre at Quiberon – a centre that still proudly bears the family name.

Between imbibing Cavaldos and cider and wolfing down majestic servings of fruits de mer, I'd learned how locally harvested seaweed has become the new wonder ingredient for Britanny's inspired Michelin-starred chefs (sweep aside the balsamic drizzles and raspberry coulis!). I had also discovered the fascinating story of the so-called 'Onion Johnnies' who each year came over to Britain from the little Breton port town of Roscoff with the harvest of delicious onions draped in strings on the handlebars of their bicycles, then rode round our country selling them from door to door, getting as far as the Outer Hebrides and Shetlands in the process.

As I prepared to put rugged Brittany behind me and enter the softer, rolling paysage of Normandy, I spotted a road sign for the little town of St. Meen le Grand. Memory bells rang. Was that not where Louison Bobet, the great hero of my childhood, and his brother Jean had been born and raised and hadn't someone told me there was now a museum there, dedicated to Louison's memory?

The detour proved more than worthwhile, even if it did take me a frustrating 20 minutes or so circling the narrow little streets of the town centre before I found the museum – which also serves as headquarters for an active local cycling club. The building is set in a leafy, park-like area, half a kilometre from the bustling little town square, with its pretty shops and busy pavement cafés.

I was glad to note that the museum has a steady trickle of visitors and that not all of them were old-timers like me. It seems the Bobet legend belongs as much to the young generation of French cycling fans as it does to those who, like me, were actually privileged to be standing at the roadside as the great man swept by on his way to another great victory.

There was just one thing missing for me at the museum that day, however. I really felt that the studious, intellectual and knowledgeable Jean Bobet should have been there; he would have been the perfect curator.

But now that gap has been filled by this wonderful book. They say a picture can tell a thousand words, but in my view just a hundred well chosen words can tell the story better, and here in these pages Jean has carefully crafted not just a hundred words but thousands of them. His story is of courage and disappointment, of highs and of lows and of two young Breton brothers who set out together on a road to cycling glory. It's a wonderful read that's just as inspiring as all those superb old Tour mags from years ago.

Roger St Pierre
July 2008

Praising what is lost
Makes the remembrance dear.

    Shakespeare, *All's Well That Ends Well*

Life in those days was so sweet
And the sun burned brighter than today...

    Jacques Prévert, *Autumn Leaves*

INTRODUCTION

I know it is futile. Pathetic, even. But that's how it is. Even though the de Gaullian reference is a bit embarrassing, I cannot put it any other way.

All my life, I have had a certain idea of cycling.*

This personal conception, which is not shared by a majority of cyclists, did not enhance my brief racing career. However, it did not prevent me from living – with dedication, with pleasure or pain, but always with passion – an experience that I would regret having missed. Fifty years on it is that period of my life which most often, and most strongly, feeds my memory.

I was an odd sort of racer. First of all, I was the kind of curiosity they called 'an intellectual'. It was written on my face: I wore glasses. And then I was the brother of the other one. That was written everywhere: Louison Bobet was the champion.

These peculiarities did not make me an outsider – I was quite happy in the heart of the peloton – but they did set me apart. It is true, for instance, that I nursed more doubts

---

* An echo of Charles de Gaulle's famous remark 'All my life I have had a certain idea of France'.

than I counted successes, which was (and still is) considered a weakness, in the arid world of competition. But it is also true that my unusual position gave me a privileged vantage point as an observer.

Though I was always aware of cycling's grassroots, I confess that most of my own development as a cyclist took place on the elite circuit. I benefited from an advantage comparable to that enjoyed in previous eras by young people of good family, who rubbed shoulders with the greatest writers and artists of the day in their parents' salons. In my brother's peloton, I mixed with the best and most renowned cyclists of his generation. They had names like Bartali, Coppi, Kubler, Koblet, Van Steenbergen, or Anquetil and Darrigade. All these characters were well aware of their rank, but could never be sure of their superiority. This seemed so insecure and precarious, while they were racing, that they always made sure to flaunt it.

Throughout those years, I enjoyed the friendship of Antoine Blondin, a regular of our peloton, where his respect and tact had won him a place. I remember the day in 1954 when Antoine, shy as a schoolboy, asked permission to go and phone his mother, because Louison and Jean Bobet had kept him at table too long.

Later on, Antoine wrote about my brother and me in one of his columns in the sports newspaper *L'Équipe*. He wrote this pastiche of Alexandre Dumas, entitled 'Lead From Behind', on the evening of the 1957 Paris–Roubaix:

Roubaix. The reader will forgive our opening the 55th chapter of such a classic as Paris-Roubaix, or the Little Queen's Diamonds, with a few historical reflections...

It was on a Passion Sunday veiled with Spring that an observer, inured to the chill wind, would have been able to make out a party of riders ranged in the shadows of the Saint Denis Basilica, where the Kings of France lie in eternal slumber. In the faces of two men, had they not been disguised beneath yellow helmets, he would have recognised Sir Louis and his brother Jean, recently returned from a mission to England, and who travelled in the guise of a junior lecturer at the University of Hutchinson.

'Brother Jean,' said Sir Louis, 'if you are prepared to hear a secret, follow me into the crypt and swear an oath, on the sacred tombs of our ancestors, never to uncover what I have to tell you, and only to uncover my rear wheel when I ask you.'

'I swear it on the head of the peloton,' replied Jean, simply.

This was the solemn exchange of two young men, divided between their determination and the respect inspired in them by surroundings into which prudence and fervour had led them.

Between the tombs of Saint Rebry and King Pélissier the First, Sir Louis began to speak.

'I had a puncture. As his name suggests, it is Condé* that gave it to me: the escort sent to take us to Flanders is in the pay of the Duke of Bruyne. Rome – or rather Cardinal Coppi – is pulling the strings. Let us feign ignorance, but keep our eyes peeled. Every level crossing will be a barricade against us, every copse of the Somme will hide an ambush, and there can be no pit stops for us in the mining villages of the northern plains. I am counting on your vigilance; rest assured, in

---

* Condé: historical title of French Princes; slang for 'policeman'; a region near the Belgian border.

return, that the care of my junior will never be the most junior of my cares...'

Jean merely inclined his head solemnly, lending him more than ever the appearance of a racer, but when he raised it again on emerging into the square, where the impatience of their steeds could already be heard, his face was lit by unflinching resolve: the young scholar had been replaced by *l'homme au masque de frère*.*

It is beneath this mask that I gained my 'certain idea' of the sport. I want to tell the story of cycling in the 1950s: a history that I lived through, and on which Louison left a lasting imprint.

However, this book is not Louison's biography, as I am about to explain.

Before it ever occurred to me to take on such a task, I was put off the idea by what happened on the very day of Louison's death. Only hours after he passed away, my brother's memory was coveted by a press baron celebrated as a great innovator in his field: Maurice Siegel telephoned to convince me to write Louison Bobet's life story, which was expectantly awaited by an entire nation. Confronted by my silence, he saw fit to add that his 'best photographer was on his way to the funeral, to take me – in front of the coffin, of course' What actually took me was a sense of deep repugnance towards such a tactless man, who cannot have known much about me if he thought me capable of such profanity.

Twenty years later the anger has passed, but still the same reluctance holds me back. For me, pouring every detail of Louison's life through the riddle of biography would be like

---

* *L'homme au masque de frère*: Dumas' *Man in the Iron Mask* becomes 'the man in the mask of a brother'.

violating a sanctuary. Louison Bobet is not a sanctuary, but he is a myth. Roland Barthes—in his Mythologies, in fact, has expressed this best. 'Bobet,' he wrote during the Tour de France of 1955, 'is such a human hero that he owes nothing of his victories to the supernatural. They are drawn entirely from terrestrial qualities, amplified by the humanist's raison d'être: the human will! Bobet is a Promethean hero.' Full stop. The statue is erected, the myth is established for all time. That is how it is, never to be changed. As we all know, of course, even if the myth is true, it only represents one truth among others. In this case, Barthes has in mind what Baudelaire called 'the emphatic truth of gesture in the great circumstances of life.' Of course, there are other truths about Louison Bobet, and I am thinking about ordinary gestures and the circumstances of everyday life. Of course...

To change the subject slightly, although I do not wish to overstate my own importance, Roland Barthes, obviously on top form during this Tour de France, did not resist the temptation to analyse me into the bargain. In rather abrupt fashion, as was his style, he said of me: 'Louison's double is also his negative image: he is the Tour's great victim. As a brother he owes his senior the total sacrifice of his personality. This racer suffers from one great weakness: he is a thinker. His status as an intellectual brings him a destructive lucidity: he analyses his suffering and loses, through introspection, the advantage of a superior physique.'

The mot juste of this passage is 'double'. More accurate than the 'twin' or 'non-identical twin' more commonly employed. If a person's double is someone who reflects him, and with whom he is in full communion, then the remark is most apt. That said, even if Roland Barthes saw the essence of things, he either neglected the detail or modified it to suit his taste or his argument. For instance, he explains that, having only a bachelor's degree, Louison is less cerebral than Jean. In fact, Louison never had any such degree, but I would like to see the proof that he was 'less cerebral'. He notes that I wore enormous glasses and that my physique was superior to Louison's. In reality, neither was that substantial: the glasses because I wanted light ones, and my physique because it was all I could manage, unfortunately.

I will part company here with Roland Barthes, begging his posthumous pardon for driving him away on the evening of the 1955 Tour's Mont Ventoux stage. Like all the witnesses of this Dantesque stage, he wanted to approach Louison, the hero of the hour. Barthes' face was not familiar to me (small wonder: how many people would have recognized him in 1955?) and I closed the door of our rooms to him. I should like him to know that I turned him away as a brother. After my day job as a team-mate on the road, I would buckle down to another role on arrival: that of the champion's personal guard-dog. It was no easy task, at the height of the competition, to keep all the undesirable visitors at bay. I did come across undesirables I found quite amusing, but who would have distracted Louison from what he had to do.

A few days before Roland Barthes, I had found a celebrated columnist from the newspaper *L'Aurore* sitting quite uninhibitedly on the bed in my room. His name was Steve Passeur and he enjoyed a fine reputation as an author of light comedies. In order to gain entrance to our hotel, he had used the recommendation of Robert Chapatte, a former cycling colleague who was just making his journalistic début at *L'Aurore*. Without raising his eyes from his notebook, Steve Passeur asked me how I went about making love during the Tour, since the womenfolk were not around. Indeed, his particular hobby-horse was to count the number of times in a day, a week, a month, a year, that a racer could reasonably express himself sexually. Luckily, I intercepted this character before he could get to Louison who, at that precise moment, was calculating – the number of seconds between him and Charly Gaul.

But all these stories are diverting me from my discussion of the pros and cons of writing a biography of my brother. One good reason not to stray into that territory is that I have neither the requisite attention to detail, nor chronological certitude. It was my friend Jeanne Moreau who pulled me up short one day, with the truth of an observation of whose origin I am unsure: at our age, we have no memory left, only memories.

An early family memory allows me to flaunt my special insight, and to claim that Louison Bobet might (should?) not have existed at all. In 1923 the family's first-born son was named Louis. Had he survived beyond infancy, his younger brother, born on 12 March 1925, could not have been called Louis in his turn. However, it was this second son, who became the first – the one everyone knows – who received the name Louis. But there was something else. Our father was thrilled, and rushed to the town hall. In his excitement, he declared to the official that his son would be called Louis Pierre Marie, without considering that these were his own three Christian names. In order to distinguish father and son, they had to find another name: a 'petit nom', as they said at the time. They came up with Louison, not an unusual diminutive in those parts. As for the name Bobet, it was not actually the surname of our father's father, but that of my grandmother's husband, a man of great kindness. Thus came into the world Louis Bobet, then Madeleine Bobet, and finally Jean Bobet.

On that note, I promise not to keep flaunting my access to family secrets. Telling this anecdote has confirmed my intention not to write the life of Louison Bobet. Every biographer is to some extent a voyeur. A biographer inside the family would be nothing short of a vampire.

I

THE FIRST STEP

In cycling progress is fast. Once you have come through the local races, the *communales*, you get your racing licence. That is the short cut; we will take the long way round.

In the old days, the *communales* were unofficial races in the sense that they had not been declared to the municipal Cycling Federation of the *Département* concerned. They were organised by volunteers of all descriptions: most commonly by small businesses who could use the occasion to sell a few more pancakes or sausages, but also by parish priests who, in Brittany, liked to combine the celebration of cycling with the feast of the Pardon. The *communales* mixed the profane and the sacred, and gave great pleasure to the whole parish. Besides, as far back as I can remember, the days of the local races – as if by miracle – were always sunny and warm, and always well attended. One or two gendarmes and six or seven firemen were enough to ensure the maintenance of public order, bringing the number of uniforms to ten at the most, and the same number of whistles. Their shrill fanfare accompanied each stage of the operation.

The *communales* were held over distances between 30 and 40 kilometres. They welcomed all male entrants without distinction of age, dress or equipment. You could be wearing overalls and riding a bike with wide tyres and mudguards. The only requirement was to have the look of a racer about you. The regulations stipulated that there should be a line for the start, and one for the finish. They were rarely the same line, because separating them made it possible to celebrate not one, but two businesses that had made sizeable contributions to the prize list. For there was a classification list and, naturally, prizes for the winners. On the subject of sponsors, I should mention that bars and cafés played a major role (the term bistro had not yet caught on in the countryside, where they were still usually called cafés), because they often helped determine the course of the race. Indeed, a *communale* typically consisted of a two-way journey along the same linear route. The competitors would leave the village and ride four or five kilometres to a crossroads – known as Four Ways – where there would always be a café. In the middle of the crossroads, the *patron*/ owner would set up a barrel, around which the contestants would have to turn before riding back to the village. A race official stood by this barrel with a flag to wave in case of oncoming danger. Sometimes, admittedly, after one or two laps, this steward, nicely ensconced behind a *bolée* of cider or a drop of the hard stuff in the café, would forget to go outside to officiate. Then, some cheats would take the opportunity to shave a few dozen metres off the course.

My own local cycling career was severely disrupted by the war. I reached the age for the *communales* at the beginning of the 1940s, which was not exactly the ideal period.

It was in August 1942 that I joined the line-up for my first race, at my home village of Saint-Méen-le-Grand. At the same time I came up with the idea of keeping a notebook in which I would record every race I entered, with the date, distance and my place at the finish. I was only 13, and came in second. 'Only second,' said my father, so disappointed that he reproached my mother bitterly, telling her that 'her' son would only ever be good for a 'medicine-man'. I should explain that the very respectable and highly proficient pharmacist of Saint-Méen-le-Grand had the shop next door to our *boulangerie*. But he had no interest in sports, and that my father could not abide, dismissing him as no more than a 'medicine-man'. To make matters worse I was a pupil at the grammar school in Rennes, and therefore also a potential medicine-man in the making. Thus ended my first cycling experience, in disgrace.

In 1944 the rumble of bombs and artillery was coming closer: there were no more village fêtes and therefore no *communales*. My racing notebook reveals that I undertook my first real cycling campaign in 1945, racing three times in the summer holidays. I did not win, but still covered myself in glory on each occasion, finishing first in the 'youth' category every time.

In 1946 I had turned sixteen and things were starting to get serious. For one thing, I was not the same youth. I had a real drop-handlebar racing bike in the place of my old upright, a real cycling vest to replace my short-sleeved shirts, real racing shoes instead of my old sandals, and the last word in cycling shorts that the connoisseurs called 'tights'. But above all, even though I suffered narrow defeats (as my notebook puts it) at Boisgervilly and the Iffendic Four Ways, I came in *first* at Quédillac! I can still see it now: at the finishing line, a smartly-dressed man in a hat solemnly declares that 'Bobet, of Saint-Méen, wins by two minutes and fifteen seconds.' From that day on I dreamt about winning many times. Always by a margin of two minutes fifteen.

I can claim without false modesty that Louison won his first race by a narrower margin. It was in 1942 at Montauban-de-Bretagne, where the race was over six laps of a six-kilometre course. Things did not look promising, since the circuit included the infamous 'level-crossing corner', where road and rails crossed at a terribly sharp angle. This spot held a particular fascination for me, because it was where I had had my first encounter with the war. Back in 1940 the German airforce machine-gunned a British supply train, and the locomotive came to a halt on this level crossing together with its wagons, which were packed entirely with Woodbines. I remember the whole canton smoked these *Anglaises*, as they were known, for months, if not years. As far as my mother was concerned, one thing was sure: her seventeen-year-old son had got himself mixed up in a dangerous business, dangerous six times over thanks to that accursed level-crossing corner at Montauban. She had tried to have the whole thing called off, but my father had only laughed, and so had Louison. Tired of resisting, she had fashioned a first-aid kit out of a little black bag, in which she painstakingly arranged hydrogen peroxide, tincture of iodine, cotton-wool and a roll of crêpe bandage. My sister and I were stationed with this bag at the fateful corner, which we were on no account to leave, in case the worst should happen. We watched worriedly as Louison went past on each lap, wearing a wide grin. The last time, he was on his own, ahead of the others who were desperately, vainly jostling to catch him. The finish was too far away for us to be there to witness his victory, but we caught up with him quarter of an hour later, bouquet in hand and beaming. My sister and I were very proud, my father excited, my mother relieved. This was the première of a scene that was destined to run and run.

In 1947 I bade farewell to the *communales*. I was now seventeen, and old enough for a licence. To buy it, my father hastened to the French Cycling Federation, or rather to its local representation, the Rennes Cycling Club. The document bore the inscription: 'Beginners, fourth category'. I was offically a racing cyclist. Licensed to race.

The ritual changed. Now, at the start of a race, I would be wearing the yellow and blue jersey of my club, and a number would be pinned to my back by fussing officials. This number validated my entry to the race: it is not until you start wearing a number that you really become a racing cyclist. I raced nineteen times that year. At the very first event I became junior club champion, and saw my name in the newspaper, which reported that 'at the finish, after a race full of attempted breakaways, the young Bobet, brother of the champion, finally snatched victory ahead of Girard, his fellow sprinter.'

Thus, right from the very first, appears the reference to my brother, the champion. Because he was already a champion, and a proper one at that, having become Amateur Champion of France the year before. In 1947, however, he was married and a professional cyclist. In other words he inhabited a different world. In fact, we were not truly brothers yet. Five years separated us and so, more especially, did our preoccupations.

As for me, I lived in a state of permanent vexation, torn between my twin passions: cycling and school, which I loved in equal measure. I strongly resented Rennes Grammar School for keeping me away from Saint-Méen and my family. I was not a boarder, but 'lodged with a family'. At my guardian's home, a childless household, everything was different. They changed plates two or three times in the course of a single meal. They listened, not to Tino Rossi or Rina Ketty as we did at home, but to Mozart, or Solveig's Song. And it was not long before I came to find these very beautiful.

It was not easy, though, and I had to keep my guard up to avoid giving away my deep ignorance. However, there were times when I let it slip. Once – I must have been in the second year, form 2A3, I remember, in the Latin-English section – they were talking about Chateaubriand at table. This conversation went on for so long that I plucked up my courage and joined in. After all, I knew Châteaubriant pretty well, having been there several times. A ripple of laughter, then hearty guffaws burst out on all sides. Finally, they explained.* I went red with shame, and wanted the earth to swallow me up.

That said, I was doing well at school thanks to my guardian, who was a teacher. I passed my first *baccalauréat* with distinction, courtesy of a flattering mark for English. My father, who had not seen a single one of my exercise books since I started in the first year, confirmed the jury's decision. 'Pretty good,' he said. In the light of my results I decided that I would not be a primary school teacher after all, but a teacher of English.

At the same time the grammar school was a tough adversary. It managed to foil my cycling ambitions. Though I was school champion, I was not allowed to take part in the French Schools Championship. The headmaster, tipped off by my guardian, formally opposed such an escapade, just one month before the *bac* exams. I judged it wise not to complain to my parents. But things took a turn for the worse when it was not just schoolboy events, but civilian life that began to intrude. During the holidays I had won a place in the national final of the Dunlop First Step. The First

---

* François-René de Chateaubriand, 19th Century writer, politician and diplomat widely regarded as the founder of Romanticism in French literature. Châteaubriant, a small town south of Rennes. The pronounciation is identical.

26

Step was an entrance competition for the Conservatoire, and admission to the higher level for the best racing cyclists under the age of 18. The final of the Dunlop First Step was naturally held at Dunlop's headquarters in Montluçon, and always on Ascension Day. I needed an absence slip to be away for three days. The headmaster once again scoffed at the idea, but not my father. This time he had been informed by my club, and contemplated coming up to Rennes 'to have words with the old fool'. Luckily, he did nothing of the kind, and a few weeks later I think he was quite proud that his younger son was one of the three boys of Saint-Méen with a *baccalauréat*, even if he had not ridden in the Dunlop, like his elder brother. Louison, the first-born, had done very well in the Dunlop in 1943. He had crossed the demarcation line to get to Montluçon in what was then the unoccupied zone, and had taken sixth place in the race. He had gazed at the victor with a mixture of envy and admiration, not daring to approach him. He would catch up with him later on, however. The winner's name was Raphaël Geminiani.

During the summer holidays I knew complete happiness, because I could cycle to the exclusion of everything else. I finished the season in a blaze of glory: on 19 October I sealed my position as Junior Champion of the Rennes Cycling Club. I won the last race by a margin of one and a half minutes. Not as good as at Quédillac, but this time it was in Rennes, where informed observers were declaring that Jean Bobet would be an even better rider than Louison.

Life was sweet. Except…

Except that everything went wrong in 1948. Bizarrely – as I would only notice much later – even-numbered years have never gone well for me. Characterised by illness, accidents, or external events, my even seasons, though not complete write-offs, have been disappointing.

In 1948, then, whether due to bravado or naïvete, or simply in order to follow my best friends, this dyed-in-the-wool arts student ventured onto the elementary maths course. It made me sweat the whole year, and it was only thanks to the excellence of my teachers (somehow I have always managed to have good teachers) that I passed my *math'élem* exams, as they called it then, this time more by the skin of my teeth than with distinction. My father had threatened to burn all my books if the school had deprived him of my success. It really would have been a nightmare scenario for a father whose other son, at the same moment, was sporting a yellow jersey and covering himself in glory in the Tour de France, where he was going head to head with the *campionissimo* Bartali.

I took part in 20 races over the course of that year. I only notched up three wins, but – here, my notebooks ride to the rescue – I was runner-up four times. It was this consistency that earned me promotion to the next class, of 'independent, third category'. I was still not satisfied, however, because my fate was not in my own hands, either at school or on the racing circuit. The overworked student, evidently, makes a tired cyclist. Things were not at all good. The rider was aggrieved that his parents had no idea of his good results at school, while his guardian, almost a surrogate parent, had no time for his sporting achievements. Between one world and the other there was mutual incomprehension. There would be passion one day, and melancholy the next. It was becoming hard to bear.

It was hard, but I do remember how the combination of sport and studies once worked to my great advantage. In the *baccalauréat* oral exam, maths students had to take a much-dreaded philosophy test. My turn came. The examiner invited me to select my question from a pile of neatly folded slips of paper. I picked one at random and read: 'Induction/

Deduction'. I paused for a few moments, and no doubt a few more, before launching into a speech that knew neither where it was heading, nor how to get there. The examiner sat patiently looking at my school report, put it down with a smile, and came straight out with the question: 'So, you are Louison Bobet's brother?' I confirmed this fact and he followed his train of thought, leading us away from induction and deduction. It turned out that he was the owner of a racing bike with tubular tyres, which kept getting punctures. The unfortunate man had no idea how to repair them. So? I hit the ground running, explaining the operation in detail from start to finish. The examiner was visibly satisfied. From the way he gripped my hand to signal the end of the exam, I 'deduced' that the mark he had entered in my report was not going to be too bad.

The strange thing is that when I told Louison this story he showed no reaction at all, as if he had no idea what was meant by an *interro de philo au bac de math'élem.** But then, how could he have known? At that age, he twenty-three and I eighteen, we were not yet brothers. But it would not be long now.

* An oral exam in philosophy in a Baccalaureat with a maths bias.

II

BUDAPEST

The city of Rennes named one of its streets the *Rue Turquety*, and the people of Rennes are still wondering why. Eugène Turquety was a nineteenth-century writer, well nigh forgotten, but about whom Charles Nodier, a contemporary of Victor Hugo, had written: 'Of all the young poets produced by Monsieur de Lamartine's noble religious school, I know of none who displays greater elevation of thought or magnificence of expression than Monsieur Turquety.' Admittedly, I am biased towards this good Catholic poet, an activist for the abolition of the death penalty in 1835 and among whose verses are the lines:

A curse on those who put the axe in human hands
And murder into the law of the land.

But I have good cause.

In 1949, around Eastertime, I won my first big all-comers' race in Rennes, ahead of the region's big names. The finishing line was halfway down the Rue Turquety. I was asked to do a sort of lap of honour up and down the street. A bunch of flowers in my hand, I was overcome by my first taste of mass adulation. I heard people shouting my name, but saw no-one. I smiled beatifically (or perhaps inanely) at the crowd, finding that the Rue Turquety was getting so long that I wanted to turn round as early as I could. And there, in the crowd, I saw – or rather glimpsed – a girl from my course at the university, equally surprised to catch my eye. I had already begun to turn and it was too late to carry on. I turned.

However, it was this same girl who, one month earlier, had found herself next to me by chance on the stage of the Anatole Le Braz Amphitheatre, working on a scene from Shakespeare's *Henry V*. We had shared the same stage-fright and received the same congratulations on what was judged a creditable performance. That is what I was thinking about when my father crossed the barriers to embrace me and say that he was not surprised, since Louison had predicted it. 'Jeannot is coming on so well that he's bound for a big win one of these days,' Louison had told him. And if Louison said so...

But let us come back to earth. I was no longer a schoolboy, but a student. I was reading for a degree in English and I was able to breathe at last. But what am I saying? Not breathe, but soar. I was free, completely free. I was working hard and cycling hard. For the first time I could train whenever and however I liked. No doubt a little more in quantity than my rivals, but with much greater quality, because I had all my brother's experience behind me. In 1949 Louison began his third year as a professional. He had seen and heard a great deal, especially from the *campionissimo* Fausto Coppi, who had become a good friend. He taught me his method and lavished advice on me, notably regarding my saddle position (his position, in fact, since there was only half a centimetre between us). We did not actually train together, since he was always away racing. However, in February

1949, on his return from a tour in Algeria – where he rode in the *Belle Colonie* at Oran, at Sidi Bel-Abbès, at Tlemcen and in Algiers – he had a free Sunday and decided to take part in a *course de classement* organised by our Rennes Cycling Club. 'Tomorrow we ride,' he told me on the Saturday night: together, for the first time. I did not sleep a wink that night.

There were over 100 of us at the start and Lousion warned me that he would sort out the opposition early on, to avoid any falls. I stuck tight behind him and we found ourselves in the lead with around 30 others, all thrilled to be hanging on to his rear wheel. As he pressed hard on every hill there were hardly more than half a dozen of us left at the front when we reached the bottom of the Mi-Forêt. This hill is the local Tourmalet, determining the outcome of any race. Louison made one attack, then a second and, without looking round, drove to the top of the hill, where he finally had a look behind him. There was no-one left on his wheel – no-one, that is, except his brother. Surprised, even disconcerted that his solo effort had not come off, his disappointment quickly turned to delight and he began to encourage me, repeatedly telling me I was the best, and that the others had had it. We approached the finish. Perhaps he would let me win this race which held no significance for him? I'm afraid that was not Louison's style, and never would be. First place was his, and the others, including brothers and friends, belonged behind. Once we had crossed the finishing line, however, he was happy to have discovered what might just turn out to be a brother in arms. All he said was: 'Well now, what's-your-name, you ride great,' but it meant a lot to me. What's-your-name, in those days, was an honorific title among cyclists: it was like being knighted. There was no doubt about it now. I was a racing cyclist.

But I was first a student. Three days after the Rue de Turquety victory I was already far from the saddle. One of our teachers, Robert Merle, was putting on a play that he had written for the Jeunes Comédiens, a troupe that before long would become the Centre Dramatique de l'Ouest, passion of the literary students of Rennes and a company that would count Guy Parigot, Marcel Bozzuffi, Jean-Pierre Darras and Philippe Noiret in its ranks. On the day of the première of *Flamineo* – an adaptation of an Elizabethan drama – everyone in the Arts Faculty thought they were at the opening performance of Hugo's *Hernani*, only with no pitched battle afterwards, just a lot of happiness in which to share.

My happiness never faded that year. I found it all a stroll: the lectures and the races. Talking of racing, I was now University Champion. Second place at the French Championships ensured automatic selection for the World University Games. Complete happiness...

With one notable exception. Louison, at that moment, was not happy at all. I saw a good deal of him that year, since I was living at his house. Every time we talked he would keep telling me that he could not understand what was happening to him. Even worse, he confided to me one day that he was completely knackered. For cyclists this is the ultimate condemnation, the supreme insult. It really was serious. True, during that club race in February, I had found it strange that he had not left me behind with the others. It is also true that he was nowhere to be seen in the big classic races that Spring. As the Tour de France approached he became more and more anxious. His 1948 performance – ten days in the *maillot jaune* and fourth place overall – had put him firmly among the favourites, but here he was, knackered. He was in a state of distress, badly needing company and encouragement. Although I had sensed this myself, I was still surprised when, a week before the *départ*, he asked me to ride with him in the Grand Prix de Nantes! I was surprised because this Grand Prix was over a distance of 185 kilometres, a distance I had never attempted, and also because I was not in training, having once again dropped all competition to concentrate exclusively on my exams. *Au contraire*, reasoned Louison, this would be the ideal return to cycling for me, if I was happy to sit on his wheel for the first 100 or so. And, you never know, I might be able to give him a hand at the start of the race. I was rather worried but, more than anything else, very proud to have my big brother counting on me.

This was the setting for a classic episode in our family annals. Enter our father, stage left. He had his own views on the run of bad form Louison – not *his* Louison for the time being – was going through. Very definite views, as always. Louison was not going well because he had become a *bourgeois* and had tasted the fat of the land: the living was too easy. Since he had bought himself a car he no longer had any idea of suffering. It should perhaps be pointed out that Louison was 25 by this time, and a father to boot. He had judged the purchase of a car essential – and I thought he was right – so that he could travel to races with greater speed and comfort than was possible on the train in those days. I do have to say that it was a fine car: a green Simca 8 that was his pride and joy because, as he put it, its engine went like clockwork. Louison had always been fascinated by fine engineering.

From Rennes all three of us (our father came too) travelled to the *départ* of the Grand Prix de Nantes in the Simca 8. The race seemed to be organised on a grand scale compared to my small-time regional events, but I forced myself not to give away my apprehension. We assembled at a transport company depot. Vast garages were put at the riders' disposal: they provided ideal parking places for their vehicles, as well as huge changing rooms. The starting signal was given, and from the outset the pace was lively. I stuck fast to Louison's back wheel, thrilled to be pedalling next to André Mahé, who had just won Paris–Roubaix, and Raoul Rémy, who had just finished the terrible Bordeaux–Paris race. I was very worried, though, that I would not be able to keep this pace up for 100 kilometres. Suddenly, Louison raised his arm and shouted to me, 'Go right, go right! I've got a puncture!' I pulled over carefully while Louison's puncture was repaired by our team mechanic – the Stella team, whose workshops, known as 'the factory', were just down the road in Nantes.

We had lost over a minute by the time we set off again in pursuit. For three laps of the 15-kilometre circuit we put everything into the chase, but the gap kept growing. It was no use. Louison gave up, and I, of course, with him. There was nothing for it but to go back to the garage, the car, and home. We found the garage all right, but the car was not there. Nor, for that matter, was our father. Louison let fly a string of angry expletives which helped to bring me round, exhausted as I was from the effort we had kept up for over an hour.

At that moment, a friend and supporter approached cautiously to inform us that our father had driven off, announcing that the 100 kilometres back to Rennes would give us some much-needed training! I cannot quite remember what happened in the next few minutes. But I can certainly see the pair of us, in our racing kit, that Sunday afternoon on the Route Nationale 137. I can still see Louison, furious at having to keep smiling and waving in response to the toots of motorists, who were surprised and delighted to see Bobet in the saddle at such close quarters. I can still see him going into a *pâtisserie* at Derval, a village halfway between Nantes and Rennes, to enter into negotiations with the owner over the advance of three or four cakes for him and, more especially, for his kid brother who could not go on. The problem was that the pockets of a racing jersey never contain any money. I can still see our arrival at home where I feared the worst, because the Simca was neatly parked outside. I heard Louison's wife, Christiane, telling him that our father had been in quite a state when he arrived and had gone straight home. This was certainly his best decision of the day. I still worry how things might have turned out if there had been a direct confrontation.

Not long afterwards things went back to normal. When Louison, weakened by a fall, pulled out of the Tour de France at the tenth stage, at the foot of the little Col d'Osquich, my father shed a tear at *his* Louison's misfortune. That was Papa Bobet all over: he took everything to extremes, but was always terribly worried about the health of his offspring. His extravagances were a source of amusement for the riders and even more so for the journalists who adored him because – what a godsend for them! – his comments were rarely unbiased.

I shouldn't have broken away so early. Making a break for it, alone, 30 kilometres from the finish, is not a good move...

Shut it. Don't think about it, whatever you do. Mustn't think at all. Keep going, even if it hurts your legs. Keep going. Keep standing up. If I sit on that saddle I'll get cramp again and fall. Keep going. Less than three kilometres to the finish now. There's the grey gable of the house before the hairpin bend to the left: I'm sure it's less than three kilometres. But where are the others behind me? One minute, two minutes, three minutes. Don't think about them. Keep going. Keep standing on those pedals, upright as possible, or the cramp will set in. When that bloody vanful of officials, just in front of me, accelerates and disappears, it will mean less than two to the finish. So… after the grey gable of the house on the left-hand bend, 'it's the steep climb, 12 per-cent for 100 metres,' Daniel Clément had said. He also said to 'hit it running, lads, remember you haven't got the right gears. You've got to anticipate it. Make sure you get a good run at it.' I haven't had a run at it and haven't anticipated a thing. I keep going. I take the bend to the left. The van has gone. No-one in sight. Not even a cat. Alone with the black tarmac. On this one-in-eight wall. I'm not going to make it. Cramp. I'm going to fall. Quick, out of the toe clips. Foot to the floor, quick. I brake and the bike shoots backwards. Stop. No, keep going, on foot. I start to push. Leaning on the handlebars, I walk up, stretching out my legs. I walk for 80 metres. The slope is less steep. I break into a run, and remount. I start pedalling. I spot Tabard. My mate Tabard said he'd be at the final kilometre. I see his arms in the air and hear him shout, 'You've won, Jean! You've won. A thousand metres to go.' Only a thousand left. It's almost flat now, and I'm pedalling flat out. The finish. A flag. The line. Ten more metres and I fall into the arms of the waiting French supporters. A triumphant Daniel Clément roars, 'You're World Champion, son, World Champion!'

I'm really thirsty.

It was the 18 August 1949. I had been in Budapest for a week with 100 other student athletes who constituted the French delegation to the tenth World University Games. The Odyssey it was not, but it was still quite an adventure. At the Gare d'Austerlitz we had boarded a special train comprising six carriages, one of them for girls. The catering was top class: the first carriage was taken up with three immense iceboxes – there was a heatwave on – and 20 crates of fruit, hundreds of litres of Vittel water, four demijohns of wine and hundreds of packed lunches. Some 47 hours later, we pulled into Budapest. Not particularly fresh or clean-smelling, but happy that the journey, however pleasant, had come to an end. We had been able to stretch our legs on the platforms at Strasbourg, Landau and Vienna, where the train had stopped for the lunchpacks to be re-stocked and the steam engines changed. On the other hand, we had not been able to leave the train when it had stopped for an age in the middle of the night, in open country.

From the windows of our compartments, we could make out flaming torches and unknown uniforms, hear dogs and barked orders, while the head of the delegation passed the instruction to remain calm and disciplined because we were 'crossing the Iron Curtain'. The atmosphere was tense, not because of any unpleasantness from the Soviet soldiers, but because of Thiam. Thiam Papa Gallo was the star of the French team. Everyone maintained that this phenomenon from Senegal would be the first of our athletes to clear two metres in the high-jump. Thiam was endowed with stunning natural class and with a *nonchalance* that was no less remarkable. At the moment in question two other factors set Thiam apart: he was not yet 20, and he did not have his passport, left behind in his room in the student halls of residence in Paris. Luckily, he was incredibly thin, and we managed to conceal his lanky frame in the luggage rack, under our suitcases and sports bags: unseen and undiscovered.

This red alert had been followed, further down the line, by a veritable firework display. Our train stopped at the first Hungarian railway station in order to receive the dawn serenade of a military fanfare and a welcome from the local populace. Then the train stopped at the second station, and again at the third, each time with the same ceremony. It was not long before the well-represented Paris University Club, with its strong contingent of Medics and Fine Arts students, decided that such a warm welcome could not be ignored, and that we ought to show the crowds our appreciation with a popular song, if not with an official anthem. And so it was, at the fourth station, that our hosts, standing to attention, were treated to a rendition of *O Balls of our Fathers*. A good half-dozen Hungarian stations were made to echo with the glory of our ancestors' testicles, and thus came to experience a particular sub-section of the French intelligentsia. At Budapest we were silenced by an attaché from the French Embassy, who put the record straight. It turned out that the performances organised in the nation's railway stations had not actually been intended for us. At the border our train had been mistaken for an official convoy of foreign delegations to the World Festival of Democratic Youth, also taking place in Budapest. This curious coincidence of two events, one sporting, one political, gave us our first surprise of the trip.

In the days to come we would become accustomed to surprises. Comfortably settled in a hotel in the middle of the Danube, we soon realised that we were in fact confined to Margaret Island. We could only leave on official business, accompanied by attractive interpreters, but always with an escort of sinister policemen. It was in such company that we discovered the velodrome and the road circuit. The cycling track was in a woeful state, and the road route was absolutely terrifying: of its 14 kilometres, six and a half were uphill, followed by a descent of the same length and a final kilometre on the flat, partly over cobbles. The finish, of course, was right at the top of the hill bearing the pretty name of Mount Liberty. This route bore no resemblance to the one that had been sent to us in Paris in advance. On the ascent, a stretch of one-in-eight (steeper than the Tourmalet) was causing panic, because our bikes did not have the gears for such a climb. In Budapest we quickly discovered that the only cycling accessories available were reserved for the Hungarian team. Unlike my team-mates, I had no time to fret. Our trainer, Daniel Clément, had decided to keep me in the Olympic Pursuit team. The semi-final and final of this event were to take place only two days before the road race, so this became the source of my trepidation. We snatched victory from the Hungarians in the final and I received my first gold medal. There was astonishment in the stadium but, in spite of their disappointment, the Hungarian public gave us a huge ovation. Was this evidence of a sense of fair play, or were they just obeying orders? We had our doubts.

But these doubts quickly faded and disappeared, because we were 20 years old, and because everything was so fine on our return to France. I did, however, have a serious existential problem. At the Gare Montparnasse I had just enough money to buy a ticket back to Rennes, but not enough for Saint-Méen. I found the prospect of finishing the last 40 kilometres of my journey by bike, wearing my rucksack, more amusing than daunting. Even for a world cycling champion, it seemed funny to go home from the competition by bike.

At the station in Rennes I was surprised, quite stunned. A delegation from my club and from the newspaper *Ouest-*

France was waiting for me on the platform. There were photos, flowers, hugs and kisses, interviews. Young and naïve, I agreed to everything the journalist asked, and even with everything he wanted me to say. When he said, 'Of course, it's thanks to your brother Louison that you are World Champion,' I dared not contradict him. Two days before my triumph my brother had indeed won the Tour de l'Ouest, organised by this journalist's paper, and everyone decided that this success had naturally given me a boost, propelling me to victory. I agreed, unable to bring myself to inform him that news of the Tour de l'Ouest had not actually crossed the Iron Curtain. What good would it have done?

It was a euphoric time for me after Budapest. I won the next race I entered by six minutes. The sports pages were full of Bobets because the other one, my brother Louison, won the prestigious Critérium des As at the Longchamp racecourse. And Louison laid it on thick. Notwithstanding my reservations, he decided to have the sleeves of my official jersey, which was white with a purple rooster, emblazoned with the rainbow badge of a world champion. This was downright illegal, in fact, because the rainbow is reserved for real world champions, not for student ones. Louison would hear none of this, however, and undertook to pay any fines that might arise. His brother was World Champion, and that was that. Not everyone was pleased with all this excitement surrounding me. At the start of one race, where the organiser had kindly given me the Number One jersey, a rider ten years my senior (though I was still very young, at 19), stopped to denounce the scandal with his bicycle blocking the road. Why should there be a world championship for eggheads, but not for boilermakers like him? There was discontent abroad.

I soon forgot about these problems, though, when the new university term began. The international student champion was far from being the darling of the university. The girl from the Rue Turquety did invite me to a *soirée* to celebrate Budapest with some of her friends. But that was a flash in the pan compared to the fireworks that awaited us. One month into the term our professor of literature, the same Robert Merle, was awarded the Prix Goncourt for his novel *Weekend à Zuydcoote*, and turned the faculty upside-down. Amid all the commotion the author very generously presented me with a copy of his book, with a dedication that still makes me blush today.

Today, a full half-century on from 18 August 1949, my wife and I are back from a recent visit to Budapest. There, as we went to look for the course of the race, we received some enquiring – if not suspicious – looks from our interpreter and guide. I think she was wondering whether I was an old Bolshevik or a KGB man in disguise, nostalgic for an era abhorred by the Hungarians. For her, 18 August 1949 was not the date of an unlikely cycling competition. Rather, it marked the advent of the People's Republic of Hungary, and the beginning of a long nightmare for her country. To spare her distress, we decided to leave her and continue our mission on foot. Opposite the still-sumptuous building that houses the Gellert Hotel and Baths, I found my route, and the bottom of the climb up Mount Liberty. Unsure, I hesitated a couple of times on the way up, but then suddenly recognised the grey gable of the house at the bend and the stretch of road, still just as steep, that follows it. I took the bend to the left. Now I recognised it all, every single detail. I was back in that confounded race again, walking very quickly now. My wife could not keep up, or did not want to. When I turned round, I recognised her as well. She looked just like the girl from the Rue Turquety. She *is* the girl from the Rue Turquety.

Objectively, my Budapest victory cannot really be considered a top class performance. The title of World University Road Cycling Champion cannot be taken too seriously. In the cycling world no-one pays it any attention, and in the university world no-one has heard of it. Its significance is thus rather limited.

Nevertheless, for a long time I found this strange fault line thrown up by my modest achievement a source of amusement. Indeed, I believe I am the only Frenchman to have achieved this 'distinction', which has earned me more jeers than cheers over the years. Amusement soon gave way to reflection. The non-qualification or non-recognition of cycling in student sport explains the difficulties and, it must be said, the poverty of recruitment from which it suffers. The school system teaches, or at the very least gives preference to team ball games like football, rugby, handball, basketball and volleyball. Sometimes they encourage individual sports such as athletics, fencing or judo, and occasionally boxing. All these disciplines are easily supervised because they take place on very clearly delimited playing surfaces and do not require much in the way of equipment. Dangerous roads and costly materials, on the other hand, represent serious obstacles to training schoolboys in road cycling. Track cycling, which provides the basics, could be made available in school, but there are not enough velodromes to go round.

I truly believe that the absence of any bridge between university studies and cycling deprives the latter of a mental and intellectual stimulus that would be of great benefit to it. At the end of high school it is too late, and too hard. Too hard, because though you *play* football or rugby, cycling is something you *do*. There is a nuance here. If you lose the ball it is only ever a mistake to be forgotten as soon as the ball comes back to you again. If you weaken on a hill, it is a sentence that the next hill will only confirm. It is so hard that it is too late to take it up at 18, and students are therefore out of the running. Teachers, and members of the professions more generally, are excluded from the peloton.

So who is left? People who dip their hands in dough, clay or engine oil, manual labourers in general, workers, and peasants. This is a constituency as noble as any other, but it is exclusive and therefore too limited. Recent market research has shown that the groups most interested in the sport of cycling are (a) old people, and (b) people in rural areas. The conclusion drawn from this sociological screening process is that cycling is a sport for *ploucs* – or country bumpkins. This is meant in a derogatory sense, but I would beg to differ.

For me, the word *plouc* resonates on two levels. I believe the word is of Breton origin (certain researchers point to the region around Saint-Brieuc) in that the root *plou* denotes 'parish' in north-western France. This is grist to the mill of those who never miss an opportunity to observe meanly that the Bretons have long provided the bulk of the peloton. However, the *plouc* is not always the bumpkin he is believed to be. Sometimes, he leaves his parish to take the world by storm. From Lucien Petit-Breton to Bernard Hinault, by way of Jean Robic and Louison Bobet, famous parishioners as ever there were: here is a bunch of *ploucs* who have left their mark on the sporting history of the 20th century. Secondly, the *plouc*, for all his faults, does possess the supreme quality of authenticity. He refuses to be a two-faced bastard, a hypocrite or a liar. At the bottom of a wall you will see the builder. At the bottom of a Col you will only find the genuine article. We will never be able to thank Monsieur Bernard Tapie* enough for illustrating this point so nicely. He had one little sniff around and off he went....

That's how it is: cycling is a rustic sport. For the various stars and personalities accustomed to a royal box, caviar and champagne, there is no place at the finish of a cycling race, hastily and temporarily set up on the tarmac of the public highway. Even on the Champs-Elysées the grandstand looks out of place, and the television cameras do not zoom in. There is no doubt about it: cycling is for the people, not for celebrities.

I am not ashamed to be a *plouc*, even if I do regret that people of other backgrounds do not come to open up new horizons and add to the 'gene pool' of a closed world whose deficiencies are obvious enough. But can we not dream? Before long, globalization will make its contribution to greater diversity.

---

* Self-publicising French businessman, politician and showman who sponsored La Vie Claire cycling team for a few years before departing for the more high profile President of Olympique de Marseille Football Club.

III

RAYMOND

As an even year, 1950 did not hold out much promise. This is confirmed by a glance at the results: for both of us. Without actually being ill, I was off-colour all year. I had punctures now and then, but felt deflated the whole time. I did 80 kilometres when the race was 100, and managed 100 when I needed to do 120. It was only after several months that it was discovered I was suffering from something that is child's play to treat now, but in those days no-one knew how to deal with it: I had a tapeworm.

Let us draw a veil... but not without noting that in the middle of the 20th century medicine in general, and sports medicine in particular, had only a limited 'toolbox' at its disposal for diagnosis and prevention. Blood tests were still a rarity, rather than the routine procedure we are used to now. With half a century's hindsight, one cannot deny that improvements in performance should largely be attributed to improvements in individual health.

Louison's 1950 season was too erratic to qualify as a good one. I am sure most of his rivals would be outraged at this suggestion, having seen Louison take the French Championship that year on the track at Montlhéry, and crowned King of the Mountains in the Tour de France. But, for the impatient rider he was increasingly becoming, this was not enough, in spite of the great promise and symbolic importance of both these achievements. To become Champion of France is to be singled out from the rest for the next 364 days, because you have to wear the Tricolour jersey that announces you to the public from afar. I should add that Louison had the good sense to win his second national championship the very next year, at the same Montlhéry circuit. That way the French people would be sure to applaud him in the national colours for 728 days in a row, subconsciously recognising him as an everlasting national champion.

To become the best climber of the Tour de France is to take on the heroic image of the man who forges ahead of the others to conquer the highest mountain. To accomplish this feat Louison chose the most prestigious of Alpine climbs: the imposing Col de l'Izoard in the Casse Déserte, and not – as can be done today – on the tiny fourth-category molehill at Trifouilly-les-Oies. As in the French Championship, there is an identification between the performance and the rider, this time between the victor and the setting. Twice, in 1953 and 1954, the same spectators and supporters would see the same Louison Bobet disappear into the jaws of the same Izoard, and emerge to win the same stage in Briançon. Bobet on the Izoard was to become an icon of the Tour.

However, in 1950 Louison came *only* third in the Tour de France. He gave it everything he had, but lost. His reply to Kubler, who had beaten him, and to the race followers who criticised him for wasting energy instead of pacing himself to ensure second place, touched the heart of the crowds: 'I'm only interested in coming first.' The Bobet panache had arrived.

His glorious defeat reflected a season full of contrasts, frustrated in particular by two nasty bouts of 'flu that put the brakes on at important moments. Louison was champing at the bit because he knew he could be a champion, but did not know how. He was 25 years old. And everything was suddenly about to become clear.

In September of that year he announced to me: 'We're going to Raymond Le Bert's.' Frankly, I sometimes wonder if we ever left.

Raymond Le Bert's was in Saint-Brieuc. I had already visited the *Gymnastique Médicale* surgery run by Monsieur Raymond Le Bert once or twice before. The surgery's waiting room was like a scene from the underworld. It was heaving with bodies on crutches, who came from up to 200 kilometres away in every direction. There were young men, too, mostly footballers from all the big clubs in the west of France.

I used to go there with knee or back complaints. The massages brought me relief – put me right, in fact – but it was the maestro's diagnosis that amazed me every time. Concerning my knee, he advised me to change my pedals immediately. The knee problems, which had been due to imperceptibly bent pedals, disappeared. With my back it was more serious. As I stood facing him, he put his right hand against my left shoulder – I can still feel it now – and said to me, with a penetrating look: 'You're all skew-whiff, my lad. Exercises are the only thing that'll put you straight. We've got a bit of work to do, you know.'

M. Le Bert had caused a sensation when he first 'inspected' Louison. After finishing the 1948 Tour de France a hero – but a wreck, nonetheless – Louison was back home in Saint-Méen, taking part, to general jubilation, in an 80-kilometre criterium. This was no different from the ones he had been riding every day for two weeks, and was supposed to ride every day for another month. I remember, however (because I was riding in the same race), how he dropped out, exhausted, just as he had done the day before. I can also remember him lying, after the race, on my parents' bed. They were horrified to find him so thin and covered in so many boils. That was the moment when M. Le Bert, in a voice trembling with suppressed rage, told my father: 'Monsieur Bobet, I am taking Louison home with me. There is no address. There's no point in looking for us. I have no telephone. The organisers will have to do without him. In any case, he's not a racing cyclist any more: he's a wreck, and it's high time he was salvaged.'

About twelve days after he disappeared, Louison, perked up if not fully restored, was back in the saddle. Whenever he could after that, he would head for Saint-Brieuc to recuperate from a big event or to prepare for the next one. But then, in 1950, M. Le Bert was appointed masseur to the national Tour de France team. At the finish M. Le Bert, won over by Louison's performance, had suggested to him that he needed to work differently. There was chemistry between them. Monsieur Le Bert had become 'Raymond', and Louison 'my lad'.

In 1950 Raymond Le Bert was 41, and at the pinnacle of his art. I say 'art' because he was guided both by inspiration and experience. University courses and degrees in physiotherapy had not existed in his youth, but he had been awarded a diploma in medical massage in recognition of the work he had done in hospitals. In particular, he had been attached to the Hôpital Maritime in Trestel, near Lannion, where he specialised in physiotherapy and rehabilitation for children with tuberculosis of the bones. Raymond Le Bert had also gained good experience of sports massage from working with Brittany's young boxers and wrestlers, and with the professional football team, Stade Rennais.

Whenever Raymond said, 'First of all, my lad, we're going to draw up a file,' you knew it was serious. I can still see those grey card files, headed *Le sport médical*, on which he made an inventory of every function of the human body: measurements (everything it is possible to measure, from the rib cage to the ankle), blood pressure, heart rate, etc. I can see them all the more clearly, those now-yellowing files, because they are still preserved by his son, himself a physio, who cannot bring himself to get rid of them. Our files were the logbooks of all our journeys.

We used our files to compare our form between seasons and between competitions: as we worked, made progress or regressed. Raymond was able to predict our peaks and the times when we would need to rest. We followed his system because it worked.

Raymond Le Bert had the touch, a providential gift for a masseur. It was a distinctive touch, whether he was giving a probing, meticulous, restorative massage after a race, or the staccato, innervating massage beforehand. In the evening, a massage could last a full hour when the day's damage demanded it. It always began with the correction of my back, because, he said, 'It's a mess in there, my lad.' Raymond's fingertips sought out the painful areas, from the nape of the neck to the soles of the feet, concentrating in between, of course, on the legs. Dead beat, sometimes physically shattered when we slumped onto his massage table, we arose purified, regenerated. Raymond himself would be as if drained of his strength. It was as though there was a transfusion of energy between us.

The massage session, a kind of sacred rite, was held in silence. When the silence was broken it was because Raymond needed to treat a bruised ego as well. He always knew just what to say to lift our spirits, usually in hushed tones, but angrily when the setback had an external cause. A ridiculous puncture or a broken derailleur drove him mad, because such incidents spoiled all his good work. Then, the mechanic could expect a proper dressing-down.

My subjective praise for the 'Le Bert massage' might seem excessive. Objectively speaking, however, it is quite remarkable that neither Louison nor I, in all those years, ever suffered any leg injury or even from cramp. This anomaly did not go unnoticed by our opponents, especially those who were convulsed with pain over their pedals. The other thing which bothered them even more, was the little flask.

As well as the touch, Raymond Le Bert had *the little flask*. In a two hundred millilitre aluminium flask that everyone called a *topette*, Raymond prepared our special tonic. The basis was coffee, the equivalent of about three cups, and as strong as possible, though in those days filter coffee was not as strong as the *espressos* of today. Raymond stirred in some bitter-tasting liquids whose names and quantities were known to him and to him alone. To help the medicine go down he added sugar: plenty of it in cold weather, and a little less when it was hot.

The little flask produced no 'buzz' or sudden energy boost, as was the case with the instant doping that was then in fashion. We took it in steady swigs, a quarter of an hour before the start, then about once every hour. Sometimes we only drank half, when Raymond had pronounced that: 'In my opinion, it's not going to help today.' Then, we gave the little flask back to him at the finish still half full.

We never attempted to have the contents of the little flask analysed. To have done so would have been at once a sign of suspicion and an insult to Raymond's integrity. Not once did this elixir cause us any discomfort, digestive or otherwise, or lead to any any insomnia. Nor did it lead either to euphoria or depression. In short, the little flask sustained us every time and never with any ill effects. It was our only extra piece of equipment. Raymond never once tried to give us a pill or an injection.

The little flask had the aura of a magic potion. Above all, it fed all kinds of fantastic speculation. That is, until one day after he and Louison had parted ways in 1958, Raymond Le Bert had agreed to act as *soigneur* to a young prodigy, quickly billed as the rival to Jacques Anquetil. This prodigy, Roger Rivière, had incontrovertible talent, since he was World Pursuit Champion and holder of the hour record at 21 years old, but he had already gained the unsavoury reputation of a drug-taker, a term rarely used in those days. After only a few months his collaboration with Raymond Le Bert came to an abrupt end. Roger Rivière's explanation was that 'Bobet's *soigneur*'s "little flask" only just gets you from the hotel to the starting line!'

To this quip, meant to be funny, I would like to add a more serious personal testimony. In 1957 I rode the Tour de France as part of a small regional team, without Louison, without Raymond and with no little flask. I finished in the same position (15th instead of 14th) and the same length of time behind the victor as when I had ridden in the great French team of 1955, with Louison, Raymond and the little flask.

In his field Raymond Le Bert never ceased to amaze, always out of step with his peers. He had no equal. The treatments on offer to cyclists at that time involved the most empirical methods imaginable. *Soigneurs* could be divided into two camps: the leg-rubbers and the gurus. The former deployed all manner of oils and unguents and confined themselves, in conditions of questionable hygiene, to massaging the legs. A few of them were actually decent masseurs. The best known was an Italian: a man with no teeth, no age, no first name, no fixed abode and no suitcase. His name was Leoni. He kept watch at Milan's Central Station, waiting on the platform for racing cyclists arriving from France, Belgium or Switzerland. In his hand he clutched a paper bag containing oil, usually olive, and a bit of old towel, never very clean. He would offer his services either for a single massage, or for two days. He worked in hotel rooms, and not without soiling the sheets, if you didn't watch out. The old boy was an excellent masseur, but he talked a lot, and his mouth was so deformed that it was impossible to understand a word. Before taking his leave he would rummage in his pocket and offer: 'Simpamina?' (an Italian brand of amphetamine). After the first time he never again offered anything to Louison, who liked him and saw that his efforts were well remunerated, as many riders forgot to do. With Leoni there were no price lists or bills. He was a decent man who made my heart bleed. When I think of Leoni, I have before my eyes the image of a miserable travelling player, forced to watch every performance from the wings. On the platform of the Stazione Centrale, with his ill-fitting trousers and precariously perched hat, he had the tragic silhouette of Chaplin's Little Tramp.

The gurus had less to recommend them. They practised not physiotherapy, which is hard on the wrists, but psychotherapy. They had a certain exterior gloss and certainly possessed the gift of the gab. They worked without invoices, but the fees they charged were high, if variable. The best known amongst them distinguished himself by his military bearing. Very sure of himself, he had managed to inveigle himself into the company of a good French cyclist, Henri Anglade. Indeed, he had won his confidence and had Anglade in his sway, if not actually under a spell. His arrival in the peloton did coincide, I do have to admit, with the best moments of Anglade's career in 1959. He was hardly, if ever, to be seen, operating his magnetism from a distance. He lived in style and dreamed of landing himself a great champion, like the famous actors and politicians he claimed to have supported in the past. Louison was his main target and, in order to seduce him, the Svengali invited him to dine in a sumptuous Monte-Carlo penthouse. To his surprise, however, Louison did not come alone. I went along to keep him company, as did Raymond Le Bert.

Our host launched into a speech about thought transmisson and metempsychosis, never once pausing for breath, and his endless babble made our heads spin until, noting our silence, he decided to illustrate his case with a specific example. 'During the Milan–San Remo, say, or Paris–Roubaix, it does not matter which – if, at any point in the race, Fausto Coppi is in your way or beating you, all you need to do is think about me very hard at the same time as thinking about him. Very hard. Now, wherever I am, whether at the race or at home, I step in. The next instant I block Fausto Coppi.' The next instant Raymond Le Bert unblocked himself to say that we did not work with witch-doctors. Our host did not start breaking the china, but he did set the glasses shaking and we were escorted from the premises by a butler, no doubt hired by the day along with the apartment.

Such are the ways in which most *soigneurs* worked in the middle of the last century: for want of expertise as well as of resources. The role of a third category of *soigneurs* of the era, however, should not be entirely ignored: that of healers and dowsers. Clandestine and illegal, these people worked only in secret (with the notable exception of the most famous of their brethren, Monsieur Mességué). This banishment from the race-side condemned them to playing a transitory role. Moreover, there was a flaw in their supposed effectiveness. The hypnotists and dowsers (I once met Jacques Anquetil's) would have nothing to do with and were utterly opposed to doping. Little by little, therefore, the demand subsided.

IV

FRANCE v. ITALY

The 6 May 1951. Rennes had never seen the like, nor will it again. It was a glorious Sunday, just the day for a big track meeting. Suddenly, on the stroke of two o'clock, there was pandemonium on the street leading to the velodrome. The stadium gates closed inexorably in front of 2,000 people still pushing to buy tickets. But the organisers did not have a single ticket left to sell. They had already sold over 9,000, more than the number of seats around the track. Unheard of. An enormous crowd had arrived very early so as not to miss anything of the France v. Italy match. This France v. Italy billing was a hit in Paris at the time, drawing in the crowds at the Vélodrome d'Hiver, where the public feverishly awaited the duels between Fausto Coppi and Louison Bobet: Coppi, who had won Paris–Roubaix, and Bobet, winner of Milan–San Remo. In Rennes the organisers had had the idea of making it a combat between Montagues and Capulets. For their France v. Italy they pitted the Coppis against the Bobets. Fausto Coppi had a brother, Serse, a talented rider who had also won Paris–Roubaix. Louison's brother was still an amateur, but authorised to take part in some professional competitions.

On the track, this kind of event is called an omnium. An omnium has something for everyone, since it is contested over four rounds: a sprint, an elimination race, a pursuit and a motor-paced race behind Dernys.

Louison and I rode well, taking all four rounds: France 4, Italy 0. The public was delighted. At the end of the meeting there was an individual race for all the riders invited to the event: both the regional cyclists and the stars. Suddenly promoted to the rank of star, I was pedalling on air and broke away with three laps to go: that is, 1,200 metres from the finish. I, this new star, could already feel victory in my grasp when, looking back on the last bend, I glimpsed Louison bearing down on me like a maniac, with Coppi in his wake. They both shot past me 20 metres from the line, and it was Fausto who crossed it first. I was indignant, and did not hide my anger at Louison, who sharply remarked that I had no right to do that to Fausto: 'After our 4-0 win, you should have understood that Fausto had to have this one!' I did not understand at all, at the time. During our lap of honour the spectators' wild applause told me that he had doubtless not been mistaken. Later on I realised just how right he had been. Was this conspiracy? No, it was a lesson in *savoir-faire* and respect for etiquette, in an exhibition race without any real stakes.

Conspiracy is something different.

Conspiracy is cycling's endemic illness: older, more virulent and more widespread than doping. Money, said Giraudoux, is theft and conspiracy. It works the other way round: conspiracy is money. Competitive cycling has money in its blood. It does not try to hide the fact, but is quite open about it. It is not creeping in, but has been there all along, from the very start. A young débutant who receives his first licence from the Cycling Federation on the Thursday, joins the line-up the following Sunday for his first race that brings a pay packet. That is how it goes. At every cycling race prizes are handed out in coin of the realm. This is official: the Federation imposes a scale determining the number and sum of the prizes, in accordance with the importance and category of the event. This method of remuneration, unique in the sporting world, is justified by the cost of participation. A bike is expensive to buy and to maintain. An unfortunate string of falls or punctures can risk putting off young beginners presented with frequent and heavy bills for repairs. In all honesty, however, this justification does not really stand up to a road test. There are other arrangements, notably through the intermediary of the club, that could help to indemnify the least advantaged riders. For the clubs, on the other hand, the troubling question is a different one: how many members would they have if there were no prize money waiting at the finish?

Because the riders are offered money, then, they try to win more of it. Not necessarily more races, but more money. Very quickly a few cunning devils get together and gangs of schemers are formed to control the outcome of races and share out the prize money. At the higher level, that of the big regional events, the pelotons are ruled and racketeered by veritable mafias. To describe their strategy (or rather their stratagem) more delicately, these riders resort to a sweet-sounding euphemism. They say that they are 'in the know'. At the start of a race it is hard to guess who is in the know. It becomes more complicated when, in the same race, several mafias are vying for the same booty. They are all in the know, but not in the same one! If you are not in the know then you are a simpleton or, in the language of the peloton, a *con*.

Throughout all my years of cycling, I was a *con*.

Never 'in the know'.

This tardy admission is not enough to suppress my anger. I do not feel that race-fixing deprived me so much of victories – a trivial matter fifty years on – as of pleasure. I cannot forgive it those stolen pleasures. Curiously, it is the scourge of doping that gives me the strength to denounce that of race fixing. For one simple reason: it is useless to say that I have not taken drugs, because I cannot prove it, whereas if I claim that I have never been 'in the know,' I can. I am certain that not a single witness could be found to accuse me of this kind of deceit.

In Brittany, where races were the most numerous and the best-endowed, the mafias made the law. At the beginning of the fifties, the St-Brieuc/Dinan mafia was in control. That was when I experienced the most surreal situations. If someone wanted to know where I was racing the following Sunday I would be asked if it was going to be 'eighty, or one hundred?' I thought they meant kilometres, but I had it all wrong. They expected me to specify whether the purse for the winner was 80,000 or 100,000 francs (worth 80, or 100 pounds). The money, and the money alone, determined the entries. Once, I took part in an event in a village not far from Guingamp on the northern coast (today the Côtes d'Armor). In spite of the generous prize money there were no more than about 40 of us, and only ten really good riders, at the start. There were six or seven who were in the know. Nonetheless, I managed to finish in a decent position. The local Mayor, who had followed the race, was sickened by the dirty tricks that had been used against me. He took me home with him and wanted to offer me compensation from his own purse. There followed a polite and embarrassed refusal.

Another time, in a breakaway group where I was unable to count more than one talented cyclist, I was amazed at this rogue's attitude. He did not once take his turn at pulling on the front, but just sat in behind. When I asked the reason for his attitude he retorted: 'All you need's a little chat'. In other words, enter negotiations, get yourself in the know. Surreal, I tell you.

My brother never knew – or knew very little – about this masquerade, and the explanation is a simple one. Simple, though never spelled out. It has not been sufficiently emphasised that Louison Bobet had no amateur career to speak of. In 1942 he was eighteen years old. He had only taken part in a dozen or so races reserved for novices, fortunately free from any intrigue. In 1944 he had followed the liberating American troops, then remained in the army – this time the French one – until the end of the following year. In 1946 he completed his only full season as an amateur, and then, becoming Champion of France in August of that year, he decided to join the professionals in September. In this way he avoided the regional mafias.

To conclude with the Breton conspiracies, I know that the young Bernard Hinault encountered the same problems 25 years after me. But Bernard looked on the bright side, arguing that the mafias were useful in the sense that they hardened up the toughest riders, and acted as a filter, letting the best ones through. This is one point of view. However, for every Bernard Hinault how many riders will have given up or, even worse, joined in and helped to perpetuate the mafia system? For the illness is still there, 25 years after Bernard Hinault.

I should point out the important fact, if not an extenuating circumstance, that these mafias never resorted to brutality or common assault. They eliminated opponents on the quiet, by tactical and strategic manoeuvres, which were often more blatant than they were shrewd. Sometimes, the mafia would block the race to ensure a group finish, because the best sprinter was in the know. At other times it would set up a false pace line behind breakaway leaders who were members of the gang. Above all, it snuffed out every initiative of those who did not belong. In short, even if it was not actually dangerous, life was not easy when you were not in the know. There were times when cycling made me feel sick.

To help me forget, I had my other life: student life.

On 7 May 1951, the day after the France/Bobet v. Italy/Coppi match, I disappeared completely from the racing scene. This was my ritual: three weeks before the exams I abstained from all competition. The main thing was to avoid any risk of a fall which could lay me up and force me to miss the June exams. I had noticed, moreover, that the amount of effort demanded by a race was prejudicial, at least in the short term, to intellectual concentration. On the other hand, I had also noted that a bike ride of one or two hours, at a leisurely pace, promoted neural activity. My method had worked in this way for three years. In early June of that year, with my final diploma in American Civilization and Literature, I was duly conferred with a BA from the University of Rennes. My path was mapped out. The faculty assigned me one of its choicest foreign language assistant posts, in Scotland. It approved the topic for my postgraduate thesis – *The Hero in Hemingway* – at the same time as giving me an appointment to prepare for the entrance examinations for teaching.

With a free mind I returned to racing, and came back strongly. I was gratified by my first victory in a stage-race: the Tour de l'Orne, which took place over three days. I often crossed paths with Louison at track meetings, where the Bobet Bros. team won many a Madison race, and Louison persuaded me to enter the Tour de l'Ouest. Or, to be precise, he decided to enter me. The Tour de l'Ouest no longer exists, but at that time it was considered the most important French event after the Tour de France. In nine stages, each of 250 kilometres, it went through the towns and villages of Manche, Anjou, Loire-Atlantique and the whole of Brittany. Held in the month of August, it wound through all the seaside resorts, if not all the beaches, thronged with thousands of holidaymakers, so many of whom were readers of *Ouest-France*, the race organiser and biggest-selling newspaper in the country.

Amongst the professional riders I acquitted myself quite creditably, even attempting to take one mad flyer which made me a virtual yellow jersey on the fourth stage. My impetuousness did not really disturb the overall winner, the Belgian champion Rik Van Steenbergen. Several days after the finish, bumping into Louison at another event, he nonetheless confided in his rather odd French: 'He's good, you know, your little brother. But he's like you: nervous, very jumpy!' Louison had a good laugh, but it set him thinking that, if Rik said so, his brother really might yet make a racing cyclist.

Brother Jean, from September, found himself in distant Scotland. In accordance with the regulations I was teaching French to some very talented young people at Robert Gordon's College in Aberdeen, and leading a most studious life. I decided to opt for total immersion in Great Britain. I hired an old wireless set which only received English stations, avoided the town's *Club Français*, and did not even go back to France in the Christmas holidays. I went cycling – for I had packed my bike all the same – in the superb Highland countryside with the Aberdeen Wheelers, who made my life difficult: not because of their cycling potential, but because ·

of their fearsome local accent. Ernest Hemingway occupied my thoughts all day, every day.

This routine was disturbed just once. Reading *L'Équipe* (my one French exception) towards the end of October, I learned that Louison had won the Tour of Lombardy. There was a photo of the sprint finish at the Vigorelli Velodrome in Milan, showing Louison reaching the line just centimetres ahead of seven adversaries: all Italian, and among them one Fausto Coppi. I was fascinated by this photo and the accompanying story, which made a powerful impression on me. A profound and lasting impression. From a distance I felt a surge of emotion that I could not, alas, share with anyone else.

At the same time, Hemingway was behaving badly. Dear old Ernest was not responding to my appeals. In vain I wrote to him on his Cuban estate at Finca Vigia, and could not forgive his silence. At 21 years old you have quite a nerve. And Mr Hemingway was clearly in the wrong, because in January I received a letter (fifteen lines if 'letter' is putting it too strongly) from a person who never wrote at all: Louison. From Menton, where he was training assiduously with his mate Barbotin, he drew me into his slipstream as well, with those few words which I have since forgotten. But whatever they were, they must have been convincing enough, since my decision was made within two days: I was going to return to France and become a professional cyclist. In order to allay my misgivings I strove to make myself believe that I was taking a sabbatical of one or two years, after which I would return, appeased, to my beloved studies.

In the event, my departure was not a glorious one. I came up with a monstrous lie to extract myself from the college, and fled. When I alighted at Menton, Louison, hardly surprised at all, asked me how it had happened. I told him that I had taken 'French leave'. The bad taste of this joke betrayed my inner confusion.

A month after my desertion I learned that Ernest Hemingway was finishing his latest book, *The Old Man and the Sea*, which would be his final masterpiece. And I understood that he would not have had time to respond to the entreaties of a young scholar named Jean Bobet. This student was now determinedly practising his scales between Paris and Nice, Paris and Roubaix, under the mocking gaze of his new colleagues, but under the protective wing of Louison, who was making the transition to his new life infinitely smoother.

V

THE REMINGTON

I received my first work permit on my 22nd birthday, on 22 February 1952. My licence was issued by the French Cycling Federation, 1, rue Ambroise-Thomas, Paris (9th Arrondissement) and, under the number 5198, placed me in the 'aspirant' category. In those days you had to complete a probationary period of about two years and notch up good results before you could accede to the ultimate category of 'professional'. The licence specified the details of my work uniform: a half-orange, half-blue jersey. Sponsorship: STELLA.

Stella, my employer, was a Nantes-based firm that manufactured bicycles and sewing machines. The company supplied me with equipment and spares, chiefly tyres, albeit extremely sparingly. In Paris, near the Gare Montparnasse, the firm had its own racing workshop – a somewhat misleading term since this was, in fact, the storeroom of a café whose *patron* had raced in the 30s. As such, he was also the team's *Directeur Sportif*. His competence was such that, to be charitable, I will not give his name. The team had its star rider, Louison Bobet, a brilliant number two in Pierre Barbotin, a valiant retinue of about ten, and one novice in the shape of myself. My enlistment had been facilitated by the respect in which my university degree was held by the firm's proprietor, an engineer who had graduated from the Conservatoire Nationale des Arts et Métiers in Paris. I drew a monthly salary of 32,000 francs, one-and-a-half times the guaranteed minimum wage introduced in 1950. It was not a great deal, and yet it was a big deal to have gained the status of a salaried employee. In 1952 half the professional cyclists had only daily contracts. These riders, who had more or less the same level of equipment as the others, were paid on the day of a race. This was known as '*musette* racing', referring to the bags of provisions that were handed out at the start of a race. It is no exaggeration to say that there were still wage slaves on the road – a good quarter of the peloton – decent blokes who toiled in vain to keep themselves above the breadline.

This precariousness of the cycling profession in the early fifties was a consequence of the brutal collapse of the market for bicycles. The manufacturers were suddenly confronted with competition from the moped. They were selling ever-fewer cycles and had to make drastic cuts to their advertising budgets. Even the champions themselves were far from living in luxury and, to keep them in France, new national regulations came to the struggling companies' rescue: the five or six French champions being wooed by foreigners gained the right to 'double membership'. For example, when Stella had to pull out of the big Italian races for lack of resources, Louison could race for an Italian firm. Very much in demand, he faced an embarrassment of choice. In 1951 he was representing a Bottecchia team when he won Milan–San Remo and the Tour of Lombardy, and rode the Giro d'Italia. The double membership ruling allowed him to double his income. The resources and know-how of the Italian firms – I also wore the Bottecchia colours at one time

– were unrivalled. As for the kit: the jerseys were elegant, the tyres did not burst (Ah, those Clément racing tyres!), and we were in raptures over the transport and accommodation. The transition from France to Italy was like the shock of moving from a one-star to a four-star hotel.

All things considered, the social standing of French riders in 1950 was half-way between their status in 1900 and what it would become in the year 2000. One detail, though, catches my attention today. In 1900 there was no advertising on cyclists' jerseys. In 1950 it was the exclusive preserve of bicycle and tyre brands, and strictly controlled: one inscription on the front of the jersey and one on the back, and the lettering had to be within a millimetre of regulation size. For what it is worth, the unobtrusiveness of the advertising suited me very well. In 2000 advertising slogans were splashed everywhere from helmet to shoes, via the sunglasses that contracts stipulate must be worn, even when it is raining. We have to move with the times. Sport cannot do without advertising; it is its lifeblood. Certain exceptions could, however, be made. In cycling, at least the official jerseys could be exempted. When I compare Louison's pure yellow jersey, free of any text (with the justifiable exception of the initials of the Tour's founder, Henri Desgranges), to the Spaniard Indurain's *maillot jaune*, with the name of the race sponsor – the bank Crédit Lyonnais – as well as his team's sponsor – the bank Banesto – splashed all over it, I am afraid that, for me, nostalgia trumps pragmatism.

But let us close the brackets and return to my professional beginnings in the spring of 1952. It is customary to warn amateurs that it is 'a big step up' if you want to make it to the level of the professionals. This is completely wrong. To establish yourself amongst the pros you have to go up an entire floor. Everything is different. The races are longer: 250

kilometres instead of 150, which means that they last two or two and a half hours longer. The speed that counts is not the average speed, which barely changes, but instantaneous speed, which fluctuates dramatically. The professional race consists of a series of accelerations and decelerations, incessant changes of rhythm which show the muscles no mercy. Finally, tactics play a decisive role. You quickly discover that cycling is an individual sport practised in teams. It is the team that decides whether to go or to wait, to attack or counter-attack with some members and not others. Cycling is an unpredictable strategy in motion.

With far too many kilogrammes (my Scottish diet had been very poor), but too few kilometres under my belt, I launched my career in the Prix de Cannes, an undulating route 200 kilometres in length. My notebook tells me that I finished 70th of the 120 who started the race, but my memory tells me that the other 50 dropped out. The race officials, the only ones left at the finishing line, had been kind enough to wait for me in the cold and gathering gloom. The winner had shown up 40 minutes earlier. It was Louison. Three weeks later I was finishing 38th in the Paris–Côte d'Azur, still 40 minutes off the winner. This time, though, my position, after five stages and 2,200 kilometres, forced some admiration from the victor. Again, it was Louison, who was snapping up everything that was offered to him. To encourage me he kept telling me I had 'passed another milestone'. 'Keep talking,' I thought, especially as the terrifying Paris–Roubaix was looming. All the accounts I had heard were horrific, involving shattered bikes and broken collarbones.

A recce of the route had done nothing to reassure me: quite the reverse, in fact. The route's blackspot in those days was the 'Wattignies bend'. Here you left a reasonably wide road and its clinker-surfaced cycle lane, and plunged into a narrow lane cobbled with 'bowler hats', in the words of the initiated. We practised the bend four or five times because, Louison said, 'You've got to turn at top speed along the café wall to stay in the first ten.' To hammer it in he added: 'Otherwise, you can forget it!' On the Sunday I was so scared that I gave it everything I had to get 20 seconds ahead and be first round the bend at Wattignies. I am not too sure what happened after that, except that I clung on for dear life to Louison's coat tail. A damned puncture lost me some time five kilometres from the velodrome at Roubaix on a tarmacked road that was as clean as a pin. At the finish, for the first time, the journalists were waiting for me. The new boy was making his first mark, finishing two minutes behind the winner. The only annoyance was that the winner was not Louison, but Van Steenbergen, ahead of Coppi. It was declared that I had turned a corner. I told myself that if there were many more corners this difficult I would pack it in. I was dead beat, completely done for.

I was not the only one. Louison had suddenly found himself marking time. For him, it was a failure not to have reached Roubaix with Coppi and Van Steenbergen. Without actually being ill, he was not well. In the Tour of Flanders, a week before Paris–Roubaix, something had snapped. And I do mean literally, as well: it was the tiniest of springs on his dérailleur that had stopped him mid-flight at the summit of the Mur de Grammont. 'Due to mechanical accident, Bobet abandons the lead,' cried the reporters. He was going to abandon it for a long time.

This banal incident – no doubt accompanied by a dose of fatigue – would plunge Louison into doubt, and me with him. Recurring tonsillitis would lead him, in agreement with Raymond Le Bert, to the agonising decision to withdraw from the Tour de France. The press reports were not favourable and pulled no punches. General opinion denounced his fragility, mental as well as physical. The most talented analysts of the day pronounced their damning verdict: Bobet would never be *un homme du Tour*.

In hindsight, I think this decision to abstain was one of the most salutary of his career. His forced retirement, at Raymond Le Bert's in Saint-Brieuc, of course, provided him the opportunity to see and hear the Tour de France from the outside, and to assess its full import. On our way to the Val de Vienne circuit for a first comeback race, we came across the route of the final stage of the Tour. On our own, at the end of a long straight road, we saw the stretched-out peloton arrive. At the moment he brushed past us, Fausto Coppi, wearing the *maillot jaune*, recognised Louison (he was the only one to do so – you can work out why) and gestured in acknowledgement. Louison was as if in a state of shock. A few minutes later, when the caravan had disappeared, he said: 'Beautiful, don't you think?' I did.

At the end of the season Louison resurfaced, winning the Grand Prix des Nations against the clock and against the rain. I came fourth. In Paris–Tours and the Tour of Lombardy that followed, we were both going strong and Louison introduced me to the world of the race leaders. Frankly, cycling is wonderful from the front.

It will make you laugh, no doubt, but the thing I remember best about that tough and contrasting year is a incidental detail that has stayed very clearly in my memory. In Sète, on the eve of the Grand Prix du Midi Libre, Louison saw an extremely flashy electric shaver in a shop window and immediately went in to buy it. You may laugh, but you are wrong to do so, and I will explain why. One of the greatest chores for racing cyclists is shaving one's legs. Shaving them is *de rigueur*, because smooth legs enhance both the effectiveness and the pleasurableness of massage, and also ease the treatment of the wounds, bumps and bruises sustained in falls. I should confess that aesthetic considerations clearly also play a part in the shaving of legs. Adonises with plucked, tanned, pommaded calves cut a rather different figure from miserable wretches with shaggy paws. It is easy for you to laugh because you cannot imagine the time and suffering that went into the weekly shaving session with razor blades. It stung, it scratched, it bled: it was a nightmare. Thus, Louison's first demonstration-exhibition with his electric shaver, in front of all his assembled team-mates, constituted such an event that, for me, 1952 will always be the Year of the Remington.

Let me take this opportunity to mention Louison's fascination with all forms of novelty and new invention. That same year I understand that he became one of the first cyclists to own a wireless radio (weighing a good five kilos), an Italian motor car (a prestigious Lancia) and microgroove records (which had just come in from America).

I should also like to note, for the record, that his house was equipped with three or four telephones. He loved the 'phone and was accused of suffering from acute telephonitis. He only had to have a spare minute in a restaurant, hotel, or petrol station and he would pounce on the first handset within reach. As he always had an idea or a project in progress, he felt the need to share it with someone straight away. Sometimes, short of inspiration, he would ring someone just to ask what the weather was like there!

I cannot stop myself from imagining him in the age of the mobile phone. It is the only time I feel like laughing when I think about Louison.

Paris–Roubaix

You have listened to the opinions of all those who wish you well: your *directeur sportif,* your masseur, your dad and, indeed, your wife. The poor thing really is hitched to you at such times. All these people have been telling you over and over that they realise Paris–Roubaix may well be the Paris–Roubaix, but it is not the only race of the season and certainly not the only one in your lifetime, and in any case…

These people do not understand.

It begins to come over you on the Thursday evening after the last big training session. On the Friday morning you start to feel a pain in your legs, or perhaps your stomach, or your head. Something starts hurting, anyway, for the good reason that, on the eve of the big day, everything has to go wrong. And you end up believing it. Inevitably, *L'Équipe* lays it on thick. On the Friday – just the right moment – you learn that the verges along the road at Mons-en-Pévèle are impassable, and on Saturday that Fausto Coppi has not been able to swallow Louison Bobet's success in the Milan–San Remo. Or perhaps it was Rik Van Steenbergen, smarting after the Tour of Flanders. Louison Bobet is scowling.

The pressure mounts and keeps on rising until the start of the race. Someone sidles up and whispers that the Bianchi team are using five-year-old, extra-wide Clément tyres, and so forth. Antonin Magne checks the pressure of your front tyre with the solemn air of a senior consultant inspecting a cardiogram. His freshly-ironed white coat also serves to remind you that you are not there for fun. As you initial the start sheet you know you have been issued a passport to Hell … and the signal is given.

Generally it is raining, and Louison is 'winded'. Not once, but three times he comes to say, 'I feel like I've been winded – in the solar plexus – don't you?' You have not been aware of your solar plexus for a long time: the only thing you know about is this bloody rain on your glasses. It is quite reassuring to know you are in the first or second group, just concerned to sense this intruder slipping in between your trusty right brake and the left buttock of the lad in front. You are rubbing along no more than a millimetre apart, riding as a single bloc. You can breathe a little better in this mass of bodies when the peloton finally falls into a regular common rhythm.

Just at this moment Louison arrives and whispers discreetly, 'We're making a piss-stop. Nanard, Tonin and Gem are agreed.'* You are tempted to tell him to go and piss elsewhere, but your own bladder is inclined to agree and you pull over to the side of the road. The toilet break goes on for an age. You take the opportunity to swallow one or two balls of rice. The entire peloton has gone by now, along with the cars behind. Your role as look-out is of primordial importance, consisting of yelling when the broom wagon appears. Because, to close the gap to the pack, it is better to shelter among the cars. But Louison doesn't give a damn: my dear brother takes his time to pee. Bernard is cursing hard, Geminiani is going barmy, Ant looks like he's about to rant, and you are tightening your toe clips because ahead of you lies a wilderness of 200 or 300 metres to make up. You lean down hard on the right, nose over the handlebars, and we're off, with trumpets blaring! This is a lot more fun because you

---

* Bernard Gauthier, Antonin Rolland and Raphaël Geminiani

can see the race at last. You had thought it was moving fast before, but you're riding faster because you catch up in no time. 'In front straight away,' says Louison. 'We're skipping the groups!' We get back in the lead and Louison says: 'Nice one, lads.' He is tactful like that. You look at the others out of the corner of your eye. In five kilometres you have stolen a minute on them. Just you wait, my dears, and see what happens on the cobbles.

And, indeed, you see soon enough. Or rather, you hear, because it's the din that hits you first as the pandemonium engulfs you. Press cars and motorbikes roar past you. Everyone is shouting because of the scraping, the falling, the bursting tyres. Everything is falling apart. The bikes have got the jitters: their rattling makes an appalling racket. And you get the full force of it in your arms.

Then comes the silence. You find yourself with two or three other blokes, in tatters like yourself. You guess that one has had a puncture and the other has come off his bike; your shoes are lying next to you. You may be a bit of the battlefield, but you know nothing of the continuing battle, either ahead or behind.

Around the bend of the next turn you spot more victims, carrying a wheel or an entire bike in their arms.

The cobbles come to an end. On to a tarmac section. You can't help laughing. Your bike turns back into a bike, tame again. You put your hands on top of the handlebars and wipe your glasses, but things don't get any clearer. You drift past one blurred figure. Someone else flies by at top speed. And you arrive at more cobblestones. Now you are sure, beyond all doubt, that the organisers are out of their minds. You bounce from one stone to another for an indeterminate length of time. You turn right and come out in the known territory of Hem. As somebody said in the distant past, Hem's a gem, because there are no more cobbles. But there is still a straight 600 metres up a deceptive false flat which busts your thighs, or what's left of them. And then the velodrome. It's completely incongruous, a velodrome at the gates of Hell. It's not right.

But you do your lap and a half because... you're in Roubaix, for God's sake! Still in the saddle. You cross the line. You look up at the podium and see Louison, flowers at the end of his arm.

Blimey, he's won it! Winded or not – in the solar plexus.

And, freewheeling at last, you tell yourself that next year...

Fifty years later you watch the race on television and realise that the Paris–Roubaix still casts the same spell. Fifty years earlier according to your posthumous friend Octave Lapize, it was just the same.

It has lasted a century, the spell of Paris–Roubaix.

VI

THE SCENE

I could not quite make out the meaning of the furtive, conspiratorial whisper I had overheard. The plan was 'to ride a stinker, a real vein-buster, to drop the idle bastards who were such a pain in the arse.' A few kilometres further on my legs were round my neck and everything had become clear.

Allow me to translate: in order to rid ourselves of the loathsome 'rats' who were shamelessly benefiting from our efforts and therefore profoundly irritating us, my neighbour decided to launch an attack as sudden as it was violent. The toned-down translation fails to convey the brutality of the move, which is a shame, because there is good cause for it. It should be known that the wheel-sucker is the most reviled and vilified member of the peloton, and the one who comes in for the heaviest abuse. He receives a level of hatred exceeding that reserved for common rats or other species of vermin, who might sit in or take advantage just once in a while

The wheel-sucker is full-time vermin, a rat in perpetuity. It sometimes happens, always once too often, that a rat wins a race and a blow is struck against the profession's code of conduct. The rat is invisible, hidden, non-existent until 100 metres from the finish, when he suddenly heaves himself into action, his one and only effort, under – if not up – the noses of those who have built up and led the race over many, many kilometres. The wheel-sucking rat plagues every peloton, under various names. Our Swiss friends Koblet and Kubler called them 'cowboys'; the Italians called them *'papa gallo'*. Sometimes, the rat has the nerve to put in a hypocritical acceleration when the peloton is cruising dozily along at 25kph. In response to such a postman's attack I can still hear the Spaniard Bahamontes thundering: *'Hoy a la bayoneta, mañana a la camioneta!'** Wherever you went the wheel-sucker was regarded as excrement. He still is, I am told.

This fury against the 'rat' is a fine example with which to convey the brutal, full-frontal shock I felt on entering the professional peloton. The shock of the language, that is. I was not especially well prepared for its coarseness, its pungency. Two or three years of applied linguistics had led me, dictionary ever to hand, into translation exercises aimed at finding the most apposite, indeed the most elegant expression. My encounter with the coarse, lewd language of cycling, then, was a rude awakening. Its vocabulary is notoriously scatalogical. In the peloton you might be shitting yourself because nothing is happening, or it might be going so fast it makes you shit, until you are in such deep shit that you wonder how you are going to get out of that shithole. A funny memory comes back to me. Jacques Anquetil, who found everything – or almost everything – annoying (and on this point I will brook no contradiction, and I am prepared to sign a statement to this effect) had the habit of expressing his disenchantment by saying, repeatedly, 'It makes you shit'.

---

* *Camioneta* is a small, open truck; presumably to take away the body of the bayonetted wheel-sucker?

This had become a verbal tic which I found disagreeable in a comrade, and rather a refined one at that. After I passed comment on this he found just the right rejoinder, automatically greeting me with a 'Makes you sweat today,' and not without adding, with a wry smile, that this was 'putting it mildly'.

The vocabulary of the peloton is a masculine one. Women, about whom riders speak all the more freely since their womenfolk are not admitted onto the field of combat, are divided into three categories: chicks, the only ones who are spared, and whores and bitches who are scorned. This categorization is meant to be amusing rather than insulting but, at the outset, it does rather offend the ears. In fact, the vocabulary can suddenly become offensive and violent because it is resolutely macho and phallocentric. Sex as a whole enjoys a prominent position. When you are busting part of your anatomy, you can bet it is not a gut. When something is annoying you, it is not your nerves that it gets on. Members of the club share a vocabulary full of members. It is also a homophobic language, which can sometimes be comical when the riders start laying furiously into 'pedalasts'. Or into 'bitches', because there could never be buggers in the cycling fraternity.

The first surprising thing is how quickly you assimilate this new language, to the point where, if you are not careful, you start to use it yourself. There have been times – always at moments of great fatigue – when, having heard the incessant talk about sods and other reprobates, I have begun cursing everyone who came along: ahead, behind and on all sides, which ended up making for quite a lot of people. The other surprise is that the language is reserved for internal use. It is the *lingua franca* of competition and training. It is in circulation while you are, if I can put it like that. When you stop, it does too. Or rather, all that remains of it in the public arena are some droll slang expressions, colourful and rich in imagery.

Without being truly elegant, the language of cycling is an interesting one. It conveys the rider's every sensation, every vibration of the peloton, prioritising the terms denoting cycling kit and equipment. Thus, to be 'on your rims' is to be short of breath. To feel as if you have 'got a flat' is to be run-down, if not dead beat. To have 'light socks', on the other hand, translates the euphoria that gives you the impression of flying. Expressions of happiness or well-being are much rarer than those conveying distress. When things take a turn for the worse, riders have a wide range of phrases to choose from to describe the level of their discomfort. First they 'squeal', then they 'jam', and finally end up 'knackered', 'tapped', or 'hammered'.

Another characteristic of cycling jargon is that it is dynamic, constantly being updated. It dies and comes back to life as environmental modifications dictate. I like the fact that today's riders no longer have 'light' socks, but 'titanium' ones. A new trend is born. On the other hand the *canette* has disappeared. The *chasse à la canette* (bottle hunt) was an insane practice that transformed dehydrated riders into bloodthirsty savages, diving into fountains or drinking troughs, or robbing bars and cafés while insulting their staff. The riders do not go thirsty any more – which is a very good thing – because they are continuously fed and watered by their *directeurs sportifs,* who have the the whole range of cold and hot drinks in the back of their air-conditioned cars. Time has been called for good on the *chasse à la canette.*

Finally, it should be known that the cycling jargon is the language of all the foreign riders living or racing in France. Americans, South Africans, Australians and other alien invaders speak the lingo before they understand French itself. Cycling slang is their Esperanto.

In the 50s cycling slang had a strong Parisian flavour, which has gradually faded over the years. The Vel' d'Hiv on the Boulevard de Grenelle was its main breeding ground. The track riders, part-time cyclists because – aside from the *Six Jours* – the Vélodrome d'Hiver only opened on Sundays in winter, used their free time to plan underhand tricks, which they dressed up in fairly earthy language. The screenwriter Michel Audiard milked it for all it was worth for his dialogues. Some of the track riders followed the horses and staked their hard-won earnings from Grenelle on the track at Vincennes. Others played at being (or at least pretending to be) big shots, becoming involved in various kinds of shady business and offering more or less dubious services, which helped them to supplement what it has to be said was a meagre income. This slightly murky existence attracted certain road-racers with a reputation for being hard men. They cultivated a *mauvais garçon* image: the bad lad who could 'use his fists, head and feet', as it went in a popular song from the 30s. In the peloton it was murmured that they occasionally brushed up against the law, which is quite likely the case. What is certainly true, though, is that you did not brush up against them in the sprint. With a swerve, a shoulder-barge or a punch, they knew how to clear the way. 'Beat it, kid!' I once heard. Only once, mind. Not wishing to exaggerate, I would say there were more crafty devils than there were hooligans. Above all, they talked big.

This was cycling from below and I could not get used to it. In my old cycling diaries I keep coming back to my one day of shame, 14 July 1954. That day I was taking part in a 150-kilometre race at Bousies, in the North of France. I travelled there with four other riders, crammed into a single car in order to save money. The organiser had not offered us a fee at the end of the race, but had allocated a tidy 'budget' for travelling expenses. My associates' stratagem was to collect this budget before the start and then to drop out of the race under false pretences. I felt uncomfortable in this role and I did not 'get down' after an hour, as arranged. At the edge of the circuit my companions were fuming: their hand signals became less friendly as time went on, eventually forcing me to abandon the race. At the 50th kilometre I 'pulled a puncture' – a fake breakdown. This is the only black page in my cycling diaries, and I am glad to have mustered the courage to write it down.

I would not be happy with myself, though, if I painted too black a picture. Cycling did, of course, have its upper and lower orders, but this hierarchy does not mean that either one should be condemned. Roland Barthes, always quick to judgment, wrote that, 'As soon as the servants arrive on the scene, the epic degenerates into a novel.' This is unfair because people also find happiness below stairs. I can bear witness to the possibility, in the cycling world, of pedalling in mediocrity and yet generating the sublime. I have at least one story to illustrate this point. It is that of the 1951 Paris–Brest–Paris, the last edition of this extraordinary event, 1,200 kilometres long and, for this reason, only held once every ten years since 1891.* Its reputation as a 'killer race' kept away the aristocrats, the champions of cycling's 'upstairs', who were more careful with their health than was the common rider.

---

* It is now held every four years as a randonnée

On Friday 7 September 1951, at midnight outside the railings of the Parc des Princes, near the Porte de Saint-Cloud, 34 competitors crossed the starting line of this race unlike all others. They would have to spend two nights in the saddle without rest, without sleep, before returning to the track of this very stadium on the Sunday afternoon. On the way out towards Brest, the race was easy – dull, even – because it was going with the wind. At the half-way point in Brest only six riders had given up. The way back was much harder, obviously, with a headwind and intermittent rain. It was cold, and many dropped out. In Rennes (the 836-kilometre mark), there were only 14 survivors at the moment when the bravest of them decided to mount an attack. There were four riders at the front at Mayenne, then three at Mortagne, and finally two with 100 kilometres left to Paris. These two were no tender youths and would not have looked out of place in a boxing ring. Both of them, black-haired and heavy-browed, were talented riders. The smaller of the two was called Maurice Diot, the larger man Édouard Muller. Both 'Momo' and 'Doudou' were cunning enough to grasp the situation in a second. Faced with the task before them they agreed to work together: it was the only way their breakaway would survive. They made a pact to stick together, combining their efforts until the Parc des Princes, where they would contest victory on the track in a sprint finish. A fine vow. But then came an eventuality that neither had foreseen. At Trappes, 22 kilometres from the finish, Muller punctured. For Diot an avenue to victory had opened up before him. But he did not take it. He slowed down and free-wheeled, deaf to the exhortations of Antonin Magne, his directeur sportif, who implored him to press on. Diot had given his word to Muller so he would wait for him. Further on, at the Versailles turning, Muller's directeur sportif, Raymond Louviot, knowing that his man was not such a good sprinter, secretly slipped him a note telling him to 'attack in the Rue de Picardie' – a famous spot known as 'Picardie Hill' – but Muller did not try anything on this last climb. On the track, after a final, epic head-to-head (and I weigh my words carefully), it was Diot who took the Paris–Brest–Paris. By a few centimetres, after 1,282 kilometres, covered at an average speed of 30kph.

But I would like to offer a different slant on the same race, introducing another roguish character from 'below stairs'. His name was Robert Chapatte. Everyone called him 'Chapatte de velours' (velvet paws)* because of his elegant pedal action as well as his talents as a charmer of the first order. However, he was also known to play the bad boy. I can still see him laying into the race director at the start of one of the stages of the 1953 Paris–Nice, pummelling him on the grounds that the race was… too hard! He was officially reprimanded, but he had the majority of people laughing with him rather than at him. They also called him 'First Edition' because as far as he was concerned the only interest lay in sparking off, or taking part in, the first breakaway. This initiative would earn him a photo on the front page of one of the evening papers which, for technical reasons to do with printing, couldn't wait for the finish. Robert Chapatte did not win much, but he was very well known.

Paris–Brest–Paris offered him an opportunity he was not going to pass up. In Paris, in the offices of *Le Soir* magazine, they were worrying about how to illustrate the start of the race, which boiled down to a long procession. The section head, Jacques Marchand, jokingly asked his colleague, the

* a pun on patte = paw

86

special correspondent, if he could think of an original idea for illustrating the piece. The correspondent's name was Pierre Chany. 'Leave it to me,' he replied. 'I'll set something up with Robert Chapatte.' Pierre and Robert were mates. When the journalist suggested that he get himself ahead a bit for a photo-op the rider did not need to be asked twice. The peloton let him go, and even had a laugh at such a suicide mission. After a 100-kilometre solo, he was in the lead by eight minutes when he turned around at Brest. It made a fantastic photo, splashed over all the papers. Nobody ever heard about the fact that 50 kilometres further on he was caught and abandoned the race. Everyone was convinced that Robert Chapatte had won the Paris–Brest!

Robert was not only cunning: he also had a gift and knew how to use it. Everyone who heard his descriptions of sprint finishes on the radio was astounded by them. Where the judges and official timekeepers just about managed to place the first eight finishers of a massed pack, Robert, at the microphone of Radio-Télévision Française (RTF), could do ten or twelve without apparent effort, and above all without error. It was said admiringly of Chapatte that he had 'second sight'. This sight was the catalyst for his brilliant later career as a television professional, and the vertiginous social ascent which brought him to the upper echelons of the cycling world.

The *Larousse* dictionary defines slang as the parlance of serfs rather than that of lords. Cycling slang is no exception. It is in use more at the back of the peloton than at the front, which explains its richness in terms of misfortune. The champions rarely hurl abuse at one another during a race. Sparing of words during their battles, they make do with a mixture of French and Italian for communication.

One thing that appealed to me straight away about top-class cycling, aside from its class, was its reserve and its civility. Not that there were no arguments, far from it. From my very début in October 1952 I was mixed up in one particularly bitter case between these fine fellows (and it is true that they were fine-looking fellows). On the ascent at Brinzio, a tiny pass in the early stages of the Tour of Lombardy, Hugo Koblet leaned over to Louison and discreetly invited him to accompany him towards the back of the peloton. Louison did so, followed by his brother and team-mate, in the slipstream of the Swiss. And whom should we find there to our amazement, but Fausto, the great Coppi, freewheeling up the Brinzio, pushed on the left by the colossus Milano and on the right by the loyal Carrea. Hugo and Louison slipped in between the two *gregari* and contented themselves with a single remark – but what a remark – aimed at the *campionissimo*: '*Basta cosi!*' ('That's enough of that!')

End of Act I.

Act II: in the 1953 Giro d'Italia, in May, Koblet was running rings around us. The French in their national team, and the Italians in their famous Bianchi (Coppi) and Legnano (Bartali) *squadras*, could only watch the insolent ease with which Hugo was riding, naturally sporting the leader's pink jersey. Always in front, he was particularly vigilant at the feeding posts, good places for a surprise attack. During the seventh stage, however, he was indeed surprised at the attack of an insubordinate Italian. His name was Guido de Santi, and he was always letting off fireworks because he could not stomach the dominance of the big boys. He reached the feeding place with a lead of 200 metres and grabbed his *musette* as he passed, dropping it again, half-emptied, on the road. The peloton chased after him, led at full tilt by Koblet at the moment when a little girl rushed onto the road to retrieve Santi's jettisoned *musette*. The shock of the impact was violent, horrific. Through a cloud of dust, I caught a glimpse of Hugo as he was flung through the air, then saw his inert, bloody form beneath our wheels. In the next minute Fausto and Louison lifted their arms to rally their troops again and mount a renewed pursuit of the irascible Guido de Santi. The latter, having seen reason, as good as barred the road with Coppi and Bobet: with Koblet on the ground, perhaps dead, playtime was over. The peloton, the whole peloton, crawled along at 10kph. After 20 kilometres Koblet was back amongst us. In the rags of his jersey and wearing a huge bloodstained bandage around his head, which was held high, the handsome Koblet had never looked so fine.

End of Act II.

Coppi beat Koblet to win that Giro. Louison, weakened by a painful saddle sore, had dropped out three days before the finish. That was where I saw him really suffering for the first time. Crossing the Apennines at the point where the climb up to the Abetone Pass begins, I lost sight of him. Was he ahead, or behind? I had decided to keep climbing when Marcel Bidot, our technical director, drew up beside me and asked me to wait for Louison, who was 'not well, not well at all.' The wait seemed an eternity. Everybody passed me, and still there was no sign of Louison. Finally, he arrived: alone, and just in front of the ambulance. Gingerly, I set off in front of him, towing him up. 'Not so fast!' he shouted. Further on he swore at me: 'Not so fast, you little bastard!' I was really having trouble riding any more slowly as we were finely balanced. So finely, in fact, that he pitched to one side and collapsed onto the verge. I rushed to help him up and get him back in the saddle, but the poor man was unable to stand, and became really angry: 'Touch my bike and I'll smash your face in!' In the end we managed to reach Modena together, after 50 kilometres without a word, one minute before the elimination deadline. It was the 22 May 1953. On the 22 July, Louison, who had wanted to smash my face in two months earlier, gave a gala performance in the great Alpine stage of the Tour de France, between Gap and Briançon. Not far from the summit an ecstatic spectator named Fausto Coppi was watching him through the viewfinder of his camera. He lifted his hand to salute him and said, simply, '*E bello, no?*' It was a strange echo of the 'Beautiful, don't you think?' of the previous year.

In their conduct as much as with their panache, the top riders had a distinction that set them apart from the rank and file. In the saddle, 'on assignment', as it were, but also in civilian life – whether on foot, at table, at the wheel – they were just in a class of their own.

At the beginning of the 50s cycling's G4 consisted of the Italian Coppi, the Swiss Kubler and Koblet, and the Frenchman Bobet. Bartali, already too old, was on the sidelines. Van Steenbergen's record was enough to qualify him for a place in the group, but it proved impossible to incorporate him. His lack of charisma, overt rusticity, and impenetrable Flahute exterior conferred upon him the role of a great mercenary, but excluded him from the high table.

The G4 was convened only rarely, unless it was in the winter at Sestrières or Arosa, because its members met all year round on the road or on the track. It was a time when the battle of the top cyclists was raging on all fronts, from March to October, in both one-day and stage-races. It occupied the whole territory: the best way to rule an Empire. From 1949 to 1955 the G4 asserted exclusive rights over the Tour de France, which went to Coppi in 1949 and 1952, Kubler in 1950, Koblet in 1951, and Bobet in 1953, 1954 and 1955. Each of the members had a taste for wearing flamboyant colours. Apart from the afore-mentioned *maillot jaune*, the World Champion's rainbow jersey passed from the shoulders of Koblet (1951) to those of Coppi (1953), then Bobet (1954). The great men were also champions of their respective countries: Coppi and Bobet twice, Kubler five times, and Koblet once. Tour by Tour they dominated in the Milan–San Remo, the Tour of Flanders, Paris–Roubaix, Liège–Bastogne–Liège and the Tour of Lombardy. In short, they were so dominant that it was impossible to miss them.

They were not just winners. Beyond their performances they had style. Grumpy commentators reproached them for putting on airs, and envious ones accused them of being socialites. In those days it was considered shocking to display good manners. So it was that Koblet, who never had a hair out of place, came in for much mockery over his comb, as did Bobet for his handkerchief. Didn't he know how to wipe his nose on his sleeve?

I remember.

I remember the day when Louison was speaking with his manager, who always received people in a large café-bar close to the Vel' d'Hiv. Louison was none too fond of the place, which was frequented by idle and gossipy riders. We were taking our leave when the manager invited us to stay and wait for Koblet, who was about to join us. A few minutes later a Studebaker – the latest American model – pulled up alongside the pavement opposite. Hugo dashed out into the rain and went around the car, unfurled an umbrella and opened the passenger door. An elegant woman materialised. Hugo gave her his arm and, sheltering her with the umbrella, helped her across the Boulevard de Grenelle. This gave rise to much merriment in the café: 'Get a load of this, boys, here's Koblet, waiting hand and foot on his fancy woman!' Louison was uncomfortable. Soon afterwards the manager was instructed by the G4 to find a new venue for its meetings.

I remember.

I remember Grosseto and Follonica, two Italian towns about which I know nothing, except that they were linked by a time-trial on the Giro. It was 1953 and a glorious day. I was wearing the jersey of the French national team, and getting worried. I was worried because I had started six minutes before Coppi. As the kilometres went by the restiveness, then the excitement and finally the hysteria of the *tifosi* thronging both sides of the road, led me to guess, and very soon to feel that Coppi was on my tail. With a deafening roar press cars and photographers' motorcycles shot past me, sirens wailing. He had arrived. He passed me on the left. He did not notice me. He was riding on a cushion of air. His long legs were whirling round and his hands on top of the handlebars. He was sublime. I strove desperately to keep him for a moment in my sights. I saw his sky-blue Bianchi jersey, the sky-blue support car in which his mechanic, the faithful Pinella, balanced a spare bike over his shoulder. This image will never be erased. One day, in a cloud of golden dust, I saw the sun riding a bicycle between Grosseto and Follonica.

I remember.

I remember 22 August 1954. It was the day of the World Championship at Solingen in Germany. I was not there, but feel as if I were. I was racing in Rennes, in a modest criterium with other riders who had not been selected for the championship. When I say I was racing, I greatly exaggerate. I was following the race at the rear, and listening. Loudspeakers, specially installed around the circuit, were transmitting radio coverage of the championship. On the stroke of four o'clock: 'the Frenchman Bobet and the Swiss Schaer are alone at the front and cannot be caught.' At 40kph, Koblet, also taking part in the Rennes criterium, grabbed me by the shoulder and shook me vigorously, jubilant because Louison was going to be World Champion, without the shadow of a doubt. At a quarter past four: 'Bobet has a puncture. Schaer is alone in the lead, with ten kilometres to the finish.' Koblet sought me out again and cried out in disappointment: 'It's not possible, Jean, it's not possible. Can you imagine Fritz (Schaer, a small man and of the wheel-sucking persuasion) in the rainbow jersey? It's not possible, Jean, not possible.' And he returned to the race. At 4.25 the loudspeakers suddenly yelled: 'Bobet has caught Schaer, and passes him on the climb to the finish.' Hugo (and I remind the reader that he was Swiss, like Schaer) joined me at the back of the peloton. He was delirious with joy. He kept repeating the words 'It's Louison. It's Louison!' Louison was indeed World Champion. However, no-one has ever related the feat performed at the same time by Hugo. In less than one kilometre he rode back up the entire length of the peloton, shook off all the other riders, won the Rennes criterium and the accompanying bouquet, and holding it out to me, said, 'That's for Louison, tomorrow, from me.'

They lived in style, the greats of that time, in town as well as in the saddle. They plumped for fine hotels, fine restaurants and large cars. They lived like stars as befitted their rank. But that never distracted them from the requirements or the constraints of a profession which kept them on a tight leash. It was a profession which they held in too much respect for them to forget, even for an instant, its spartan discipline. The surprising thing is that the top riders did not live as a race apart. They were popular and enjoyed mingling with the crowd, even if they sometimes had to watch out for the odd uncontrolled rush or over-zealous embrace. They signed hundreds of photos at the start and the finish of their races. Even amid the wildest confusion, they could greet a lady, reply to journalists, and smile to their admirers. Put simply, they had class, and the public appreciated it. They were the champions next door. You could touch them, talk to them.

Now let me share a confidence: the attitude of today's champions, kept away inside fortress buses with tinted windows, parked in special reserved areas out of bounds to ordinary people, sends a chill down my spine.

Le manager

He had the dough. In other words, even if that is all he had, he had everything.

Daniel was a manager (pronounced *manadgère*). He was *the* manager, even, because there were no others.

In the 50s, when official cycling, that of the real, big races, was unable to feed its men properly, exhibition cycling, that of the criterium and the velodrome, was making hay. The manager reigned unopposed over this branch of cycling, and his power was greater than that of the Presidents of the ICU and the French Federation. He was responsible for easily 100 events. He drew up the calendar, the cast list and, of course, the prizes. The line-up consisted of the riders he had under contract, a good 50 of them, and obviously the very best – the ones who won or caught the eye in the big events. The manager/rider contract was uniquely simple. For every engagement signed for the manager deducted ten per-cent of the rider's fee.

All except for Louison, who had a special relationship with the manager. While the other riders, almost without exception, called him 'Monsieur', Louison was on familiar terms with him as 'Daniel'. The latter, with his innate cunning, had only just arrived on the scene when he was the first to sense, as early as 1948, that this Louison Bobet was the one to back. He had the intuition of a horse dealer, without the dishonesty. As he was another stickler for doing a proper job, he got on royally with Louison, who always showed great respect and professionalism towards the organisers and the public. At the end of every season Louison and Daniel settled their business amicably after a dinner paid for by Daniel, much to the astonishment of the entire world of cycling, where the tightness of the manager's wallet was legendary.

This wallet was well-stocked.Through the sweat of the riders, according to his enemies, who were legion, but also thanks to his honest qualities. A terrifically hard worker, blessed with an extraordinary gift of the gab, he had built up solid networks among race organisers in the farthest provinces, but also among the senior officials, bicycle manufacturers and, of course, the riders themselves. To these, his dear riders, he offered for each event a sum roughly equal to their monthly salary. He had the art of forming consensus, enabling him to bring together on the same billing Coppi, Kubler, Van Steenbergen, Bobet and the others who were at each other's throats all year round. He could not abide conflict or complaints and the money greatly eased the process of avoiding them. In this world, his world, he was like a fish in water. Once again, he sensed Bobet's decline before anybody else, and signed Anquetil. This was a master-stroke because Jacques proved as assiduous as Louison had been in fulfilling his obligations at the track meetings and criteriums.

Just one cloud, by the name of Poulidor, had momentarily cast its shadow over him. On the advice of his *directeur sportif*, Antonin Magne, Poulidor signed up with another manager, Roger, who looked after the malcontents and the rejects. As Roger was also very good, he drew a certain number of genuine champions into his fold. The competition put an end to the monopoly and the riders' situation was greatly improved.

At the same time Daniel was hunting lucrative game in other fields. When the bicycle manufacturers were given permission to associate with firms outside the sport, Daniel's talents worked wonders. No-one else was as good at unearthing the capital necessary for the creation of big teams. He broke down doors and forced his way into negotiations with *apéritif* and car brands, the big supermarkets and makers of lubricants. I have to recognise that, at the same time, he won the admiration of everybody he talked with; they were fascinated by such an intelligent, yet uneducated, character. With a vocabulary that was not only limited but also rather approximative, he argued his case with such enthusiasm and in such a fashion that, either taken aback or exhausted by his speeches, the captains of industry would give their assent.

I had some difficulties with Daniel from the outset. He knew me to be too polite to pull him up over a gross error of grammar, but he knew that I knew. Hence a certain lack of trust towards me.

Dark and handsome, the manager took pride in his appearance; his elegance reminded me of an Argentinian tango dancer. One day he summoned me in order to give me some sartorial advice, judging that my suits and ties were as dull as a professor's and that this did not sit well with the public. I looked at him coldly. He never raised the issue again. Later on he had a nasty scare – he was prone to scares – when I initiated, in response to a call from the leading lights of the peloton, the creation of the Union of Professional French Cyclists. Our organisation was designed to be independent of all the bodies that made up the world of cycling, including his own. Given that the press was, at that very moment, denouncing his hegemony and demanding that his activities be regulated, he toned down his objections considerably.

I never believed that this man could jeopardise the honour of our sport. I assured his detractors that his common sense prevented him overstepping the bounds of what was reasonable. This was a very good thing, because he very often came into contact with unreasonable people. In Italy, notably, little princes from Lombardy who had made their fortune in vermouth, salami, household appliances or indeed in tagliatelle were tearing one another to pieces as they vied to buy up the champions, and they inevitably addressed themselves to Daniel, whose head was set spinning by the millions of *lire* they had to offer.

In Milan in October 1959 Daniel was carrying in his strongbox four enormous 'Italian' contracts for Anquetil, Bobet, Darrigade and Rivière. In other words, he had in his hands the future or the disappearance of French cycling. At that time I was starting out in journalism, having until recently been a rider myself. In the courtyard of *La Gazzetta dello Sport* Daniel gestured to me to follow him to a first-floor office. With the contracts tucked under his arm, all he said was: 'I can't do it. What do you think?'

At that moment I gave him a look as warm as my earlier one had been frosty.

The next day the manager refrained from selling French cycling to the Italians.

VII

THE RAINBOW

The luminescent phenomenon we call a rainbow appears as a sign that, after the rain, fine weather is on its way. In 1954 the fine weather was represented by Louison in his World Champion's jersey. The rain beforehand was me.

I hesitated for a long time before embarking on this mysterious digression. It is an episode that not only concerns my humble person but, in its own way, also sheds light on French life at that time. Let us digress then. I have so far neglected to mention that, in 1953, I was in the army. It slipped my mind because you could hardly tell the difference. Appointed to the Armed Forces Sporting Centre that would soon become known as the Joinville Battalion, I was given complete freedom to train and take part in all the races. For the Giro d'Italia I had no need to ask permission. My selection for the France team ensured that I was sent there on mission. Such favourable treatment was no mean advantage, especially as military service lasted 18 months and extended over two sporting seasons. In the 11th month precisely, the Sporting Centre fell under a ministerial decree that forbade it from accepting professional athletes into its ranks. Fortunately, I was transferred to headquarters, the Gouvernement Général, at the Hôtel des Invalides in Paris.

I wore uniform three mornings a week, in order to give English lessons to officers preparing for the École Supérieure de Guerre. Otherwise, I was still living with my parents and calmly making preparations for my wedding day, scheduled for mid-November. On my return from wedding leave my direct superior – only General Zeller, the military governor of Paris! – summoned me into his vast office overlooking the Esplanade des Invalides. Attention! At ease. 'Sit down, Bobet. Do you know Germany?'

'No, Sir.'

'Well, you soon will. I have here, on my desk, a transfer order in your name. You are going out immediately to join the 7th Regiment of Moroccan Tirailleurs. They are stationed at Giessen, not far from Frankfurt. I realise you will be disappointed: it's not an ideal honeymoon. But do not forget, Bobet, that in the army orders are to be carried out. A change of orders comes later, and I shall see to that personally.'

When, five days into married life, I found myself and all my kit on the night train to Frankfurt, bound for a regiment whose existence I had never suspected, I had the strong impression that I was being punished for something, despite assurances to the contrary from the General in command of Paris. When, from Giessen, I was transferred to Marburg, to the regiment's 3rd Battalion, I feared the worst because this place was even more isolated and because, on my arrival, the officers gave me looks that were suspicious at best, and at worst threatening. I understood why: a transferred soldier leaves with his kitbag, but not his papers. The papers 'follow'. In the meantime the officers of the Moroccan regiment, recently back from Indochina and preparing to return there, were asking themselves why this waster had landed in their unit.

Back in Paris Louison, as worried as he was furious, rang Jacques Goddet, proprietor of *L'Équipe* as well as director of the Tour, who rang the Minister of Defence. As luck would have it, the Minister also hailed from Brittany. His name was René Pleven, but we would never actually meet him. His private secretary, assigned to look into my case, was also a Breton. An irritated Breton because, though he wanted to be affable, it was clear from his tone that the case was a serious one. It appeared from my dossier that I was guilty of Communist activities and considered to be a deserter! Regarding the desertion charge, it was reported that one Sunday in November I had taken part in a Belgium/France match at the Velodrome d'Hiver in Brussels, without having obtained the necessary permission. This accusation was quickly dismantled because that particular Sunday had in fact been the only one that I spent on guard duty at the Invalides. Slowly, very slowly, the investigation took its course.

In Marburg the atmosphere was eased by the arrival, and the perusal, of my papers. It turned out that Private Bobet was not a criminal after all, just a lad who aroused some curiousity, even sympathy. He was also a young man of 23, unhappy, as you can imagine, separated from his wife, and discovering an unknown world: the army. My direct superior, the company's warrant officer, who was from Alsace, called me over one day: 'Here, Bobet, I'm leaving you the keys with the Colonel's agreement. You're taking my place. You know what to do, I've been watching you. You can also have my orderly, Mohamed. I'm off on leave: I've got 40 days overtime to take. I'm putting my faith in you.' I have never forgotten the handshake of this man – his name was Weiss, I recall – who had not seen his mother for two years and risked not seeing her again for a long time. That was the day I got to know the army.

That said, I did manage to provide some services to the regiment, because the local shooting range was shared with the British army which had also been 'occupying' Germany since 1945. You know what, lads? Bobet speaks English. I also provided the Moroccan Tirailleurs with a day of glory in Marburg. In a ping-pong competition that brought together all the units stationed in the territory I won the final by beating an officer of the Dragoons. That evening, the 'Arabs' made merry in Marburg and sang the health of Tirailleur Bobet, who had vanquished the Dragoon. However, I did even better off duty. In three months I taught Mohamed, my guardian angel, to read. Mohamed would wake me every morning with a cry of 'Boubie, get up, dammit, the Colonel he arrives!' Teaching French to this Moroccan in Germany, who was bedazzled by his new-found knowledge, remains an important memory of my youth. It only remains for me to tell you how the affair ended.

At the beginning of 1954 Louison Bobet and the others were training and disputing the first races of the season. Without me. It was not until the end of March that the case of Private Jean Bobet reached its conclusion. It was the most unexpected, the most comical and extravagant *dénouement*, which arrived in the form of a telegram: Private Jean Bobet is to report immediately to Dupleix Barracks in Paris. Signed, René Pleven. When I presented myself at the barracks in question I was relieved of my kit and, at the same time, of my military obligations, a fortnight before the other recruits who had been called up at the same time. Shortly after my 'liberation' Mohamed and his countrymen embarked for Indochina once again. It was just before the defeat at the Battle of Dien Bien Phu.

Twenty years later I humbly sought clarification of the details of my story from M. René Pleven. The old man did not deign to respond. So I never knew, and never will. My personal belief is that it was the 'Communist activities' (in a family that venerated de Gaulle) mentioned in my dossier, that tipped the balance. Allow me to divulge that in 1952, following a meeting with Louis Aragon, whom he had naturally found very charming, the student cyclist had delivered two or three sporting stories to the journal *Les Lettres Françaises*.* In 1952 that student cyclist did not know that the witch-hunt led by the American Senator McCarthy would not spare the French, or at least certain circles in France.

End of story.

Or is it? In 1953 the Gaullist Louison Bobet was certainly not the ideal intermediary to mount the defence of his allegedly Communist brother. Had he not signed the Stockholm Appeal, a manifesto launched by the World Peace Council in 1950 and supported by the USSR and the Communist Parties? His name did indeed figure among the signatories, although he had never actually made any such engagement himself. We always believed that the petition must have been slipped under his pen among dozens of other papers, in the crush of an autograph session, at the start or finish of a race.

The very next day after my liberation I was back on my bike. I trained fanatically for two weeks, obsessed by the idea of making up for the time I had lost. Louison had cooked up a gentle comeback for me, on the track with him in Brittany. We raced three times in the week of 18 April. On 25 April,

---

* Louis Aragon, poet and novelist and a prominent Communist intellectual, was editor of *Les Lettres Françaises*, the literary supplement of the Communist daily newspaper *L'Humanité*.

at Redon, in a race behind Dernys, I fell. It was a very nasty fall and I was taken straight from stretcher to ambulance and hospital. I had sustained a fracture – just a hairline, truth to tell – in my right hip. I suffered the greatest damage when I got the bill. Raymond Le Bert was categorical: I was to be out of action for two months. After immobilization, physiotherapy and returning to training, I took my place in the peloton once more, but I could only play bit parts. And I could not prevent myself from cursing this new even-numbered year. By sticking doggedly at it – I never abandoned a race – I was finally looking like a racing cyclist again in the run-up to the Tour de France. I watched the *Départ*, because, logically, I was not invited.

Nonetheless, I still managed to see that race from the inside because I took part here and there in *réunions d'attente** held in the towns on the route of the Tour. I saw Louison win in Lille: in the sprint, but above all by sheer power. It was only the second stage, but I sensed that the favourite was already perceived as the probable victor. I saw him again in Lyon, wearing yellow after a difficult crossing of the Massif Central which, he told me, had 'knackered a fair few'.

Most importantly, I saw the Grenoble–Briançon stage and the Col de l'Izoard. What I saw, in the lunar landscape of the Casse Déserte, was everyone else behind and Louison in front, far ahead. He was climbing fluidly and at speed. Limpid and lucid at the same time. He came over to me as he passed to ask where Christiane was. Christiane, his wife, rarely seen on the route of the Tour de France, was 200 metres further up. Fine. He ran his fingers through his hair, took the time to spruce himself up, and got back to the business in

---

* A criterium or track race held in the stage-finish town before the arrival of the Tour

hand on a one-in-ten climb! Louison dominated that Tour. Ferdi Kubler, the runner-up, finished more than a quarter of an hour behind him in the overall placings in Paris. At the Parc des Princes, where he received a triumphal welcome, I no longer recognised him. He had been liberated; Louison the worrier had become a warrior. He let himself go so far as to confide: 'I tell you, I'm cruising.' He was a different man.

The cruise of this happy man would last until the end of the year. In the month of August, as I have already said, he was crowned World Champion in Solingen in Germany, to the strains of the *Marseillaise*, surrounded by the occupying French troops. In patriotic fervour he threw the gladioli from his bouquet towards the nearest of the soldiers who were pressing round him. Some 30 years later, in Biarritz, I would receive a visit from a couple of young retirees from Normandy. From her bag the woman pulled out a dried flower. 'This is the flower your brother threw to my fiancé, who sent it straight to me. In my village my fiancé was "the man who saw Bobet". We kept the flower ever since, but we are happy to present it today to the museum that bears his name.'

Testimonies like this one, involving shared bouquets, or attentions paid to sick or disabled people, are memories that persist. They still bring them to me through the intermediary of their children. Thus, every year, on 1 January, 12 March (his birthday) and 25 August (Saint Louis' Day), a very elderly mother thanks me with the same simple words, because Louison welcomed her son, who was suffering from polio, into his home . The son was 16 years old and is now in his 60s.

The most remarkable memory, because it is the best-known, is that of a boy aged 16 or 17 who, 25 years later, remembered asking Lousion for his autograph. The boy's name was Georges Perec*, and in his first-rate collection *Je me souviens*, he writes his memory number 17:

'I remember getting the autograph of Louison Bobet at the Parc des Princes.'

The young Perec must have been a devoted fan because he also writes, in memory 138:

'I remember that Jean Bobet – brother of Louison – had a degree in English.'

It is the strangest thing to hear the actor Sami Frey saying these lines of Perec today, on the stage, as though they were his own.

I digress, no doubt, but I do have an excuse. It is that from September 1954, everything changed. Louison entered another dimension.

First, he altered his professional status by leaving the little Stella team in Nantes for the big Mercier team in Saint-Étienne. He signed two contracts with his new manufacturers: one racing contract and one commercial one. The firm Mercier undertook to produce and sell bicycles under the brand name Louison Bobet. The bike of the Louison Bobet team, a Mercier subsidiary, was yellow, as was its jersey, bearing only the inscription Louison Bobet–Hutchinson, in blue letters. It was advertising with restraint.

My own new contract appeared complicated, to say the least. On top of the usual clauses about the rights and reponsibilities of the rider and the employer was a long chapter stipulating that I was forbidden from producing or having cycles and other accessories manufactured under the Bobet name. Such a level of precaution seemed pointless and clumsy more than anything else, so I opened my heart about it to the intransigent M. Mercier in person. 'You ought

---

* highly regarded experimental novelist and essayist

to know,' he informed me, thumbs tucked firmly into the waistcoat of his three-piece suit, 'you ought to know, my dear Jean Bobet, that in this life one cannot be too prudent.' Twelve months later at the 1955 Cycle Show, M. Mercier discovered a new competitor on the exhibition stand right next to his own, promoting the brand 'Louison'. Its registered office was also in Saint-Étienne. When I joked to M. Mercier, who was an affable man but devoid of humour, that I was preparing to register the 'Jeannot' brand, he took my remark literally. Business is business.

When I say that everything changed from September 1954 I mean that this change had repercussions beyond the small world of cycling. Louison the cycling champion suddenly became a star. He was on the front pages, he was photographed at Studio Harcourt (one day, I remember, he bumped into the beautiful actress Michèle Morgan there and was struck dumb in admiration), he was snapped up for advertisements. Everybody wanted a piece of him. Whenever the requests were unusual or tricky he would ask for my opinion. He had to consult me about how to respond to the journalist who asked him what he would take to a desert island, simply because he could not imagine himself being away from his world, even for a moment.

He was soaring. In more ways than one, since we were spending a good deal of time in the air. We travelled by 'plane (in 1954 the aeroplane, Air France and its icon the *Pégase* were the height of chic) because Morocco, Portugal and England all wanted Bobet to visit.

We raced in Casablanca, in the fine Anfa velodrome, where we roused an already over-excited public, immediately realising that it would only be fitting to beat the Moroccan line-up in a close-run competition, by two victories to one. Three days later we were turning out in Lisbon, (I trust you understand whom I mean when I say 'we') in front of 30,000 spectators who had come to cheer four riders: the World Champion and his team-mate pitted against two Portuguese riders. I note from my diary that their names were Reposo and Pereira, but I am unable to put faces to them. It does not matter because it was no ordinary show that the Sporting-Club of Lisbon had in store for its members that evening. They wanted an hour and a half of laps of honour from Louison, in a stadium that was conquered in advance. It was followed by a night that I remember very well. The Sporting Club led us to a nightclub, 'The Machado', as I recall. This was where the fashionable set of Lisbon in the Salazar era came, in numbers, to pay homage to the local idol, the singer Amalia Rodrigues, and the strains of the *fado** continued late into the night.

Another exhibition race, for which I myself was partly responsible, took us to London. Louison had agreed to present the year's trophies to Britain's cyclists – men and women in evening dress, if you please – at a prestigious ceremony in the Royal Albert Hall. In the royal box with our wives, I was bowled over by this conclusion to a fantastic (though even) year, with a most unexpected image of Louison: on the great stage of this grand hall, listening religiously to *God Save the Queen* (much to his delight, because he and the Queen were the same age) and joining in that traditional farewell song, *Auld Lang Syne*, which the English are the only ones to sing with such fervour.

---

* mournful style of Portuguese folk song of which Amalia Rodriguez was a great exponent

A short digression. On my return to Paris I set myself a personal challenge. In order to exorcise the demons of Redon, that terrible mash of fallen bikes and motorcycles, I decided to mount an attack on the local hour record at the Vel d'Hiv, behind a Derny. I beat the record, with a distance of 54 kilometres, 884 metres.

Above all, I regained my appetite.

In January 1955 the English gave us a surprise once again. Not the amateurs from the Royal Albert Hall, but some unexpected professionals. They disembarked near Sainte-Maxime on the Mediterranean coast, more precisely in the inlets of Issambres, where we had our training camp. There were a dozen of them, true pioneers of British professional cycling, making up a solid and ambitious team that bore the lofty name of Hercules. We met them from time to time, on the tortuous roads that cross the hinterland of the Var. Poking out of the back pocket of their jerseys was the Michelin map that was at once a passport and a letter of introduction in this strange and unknown land. My colleagues subjected them to more or less friendly teasing, but I made sure not to display the least arrogance. Having studied the market I knew that Hercules manufactured five times more bicycles than did Mercier, and that British cycle production was ten times greater than that of France. I was happy, besides, to offer my services to the new arrivals as an interpreter, but my initiative quickly proved unnecessary. One month after their arrival I bumped into their leader, one Brian Robinson, who, in fine colloquial French came straight out with: 'We were hellish peckish yesterday, but today we picked up some grub.' *Les Anglais* had understood everything: they spoke the lingo.

Louison and I did not speak much, as usual, although we were riding a good deal more than usual. We avoided the company of groups who tended to chat and dawdle. This was the time of year that Raymond Le Bert was at his most productive. He kept his files up to date (weight, blood pressure, heartbeat before and after exercise…), comparing them to those of the previous year. The same regime was observed. When our mileometers read 1,200 kilometres we thought we were the greatest, capable of facing any competition. And Raymond had a good laugh, because he knew what was coming next. We hit a rocky patch, the bleak period between 1,500 and 2,500 kilometres. Then, little by little, we came out of it, full of beans again. Raymond had another laugh: 'It's hard work that pays off, kids, it's the work.' In the pre-season races we checked that we were up to speed and, between ourselves, 'a little bit more than up to speed'. We were careful not to give away our confidence in front of the journalists who came to visit, and of whom there were more than ever that year. From our interviews with the classiest of them – Maurice Vidal from *Miroir Sprint*, Jacques Marchand from *L'Équipe*, Ruggero Radice from *Tuttosport*, and André Costes from *France-Soir* – we came to understand that people were awaiting the new Bobet brothers with as much curiosity as impatience.

The new Bobets appeared on 12 March (Louison was 30, believe it or not) at the start of the Paris–Nice, the obligatory season-opener. Beneath the Eiffel Tower, and in temperatures of minus four degrees, we met our new *directeur sportif,* Antonin Magne.

I must say a few words about M. Magne. Sparing of words (and with everything else, according to malicious gossip) Antonin Magne stood out on the frenetic racing scene by virtue of his courtesy and his wisdom. He wore a white coat, a purple scarf (the Mercier colours) and a Basque-style beret. He always addressed his riders formally, though the relationship was a close one. He had his methods: long training sessions, for example, and he demanded that they be applied to the letter. However, at our first ever meeting in his austere office on the Avenue de la Grande-Armée (a long way from the bistro storeroom in Montparnasse) he was very clear with Louison: 'I know that your method – training in short bursts – is different, and it has yielded results. Antonin Magne is not going to teach Louison Bobet any lessons, but he is counting on Louison Bobet. You have my complete confidence.' At Issambres he wrote to us once, just once, but it meant a great deal. On his official notepaper, bearing the motto 'No glory without virtue', he offered Louison his programme for the first part of the year, and asked in passing how the training kilometres were going.

In Paris, underneath the Eiffel Tower, just after starter's orders had been given, he asked Louison and me to stay close to him. He looked us over, or rather scrutinised us at length, from head to foot and back again, and finally made up his mind: 'I see you're both in excellent form.'

Little did he know how right he was. Five hours later, approaching Nevers, where the first stage ended, I left everyone behind and found myself alone out in front. For 20 kilometres I had time to dream, to doubt and then to believe in my chances. I was shown my lead: more than a minute! My head was in turmoil: I'm the best … they're bound to catch me … but no, I really am looking good. The only regret was that Antonin Magne was not there to witness my triumph. He turned up by my side three kilometres from the finish. He leaned out of his car and I waited for the flood of encouragement, the torrent of congratulations that is *de rigueur* in such circumstances. Then Antonin Magne spoke: 'Good, Jean. Keep some for tomorrow.' Monsieur 'Tonin' was sparing with his praise.

After that, everything fell into place. I won Paris–Nice and came third in Milan–San Remo, where it was said that I had pulled off the exploit of the day with a lone break of 40 kilometres. Louison won the Tour of Flanders, ahead of Van Steenbergen and Koblet. As we had arranged, we took time off in May. On his return Louison was in supreme form. He won the Tour of Luxembourg from the local hero, Charly Gaul, and then destroyed everybody to take the Dauphiné Libéré. At the finish of the eighth and final stage in Grenoble, Antonin Magne gathered the whole team together in the lounge of our hotel and requested that we wait for Louison, who had been delayed by his victor's duties. When Louison appeared Antonin Magne ordered, 'Please stand, Messieurs. You are in the presence of a great champion.' Monsieur 'Tonin' also knew how to give praise generously.

Everything went beautifully until the French championship, which was held at Châteaulin, in Brittany. In the sprint Louison was beaten by a whisker, just ten centimetres, by André Darrigade. This interruption to the flow of his victories took him by surprise; Louison was furious. He threatened to lodge a complaint against his victorious opponent for taking what he thought was an irregular line in the sprint. I caught up with him far beyond the finishing line, where there were no spectators. I had great trouble calming him down. 'Look at yourself,' I snapped eventually. 'Can you see yourself? With the World Champion's jersey on your back you're going to quibble over the French Champion's one?' It was as if I had punched him in the stomach. He heard reason. Our eyes met those of the only witness to this scene, a reporter from the *Parisien Libéré* named André Chassaignon, whom I hardly knew. He had the good taste not to relate this scene until a month later, after the Tour de France.

Because the Tour was going to start in ten days.

*1. Louison in the time trial stage in the 1950 Tour de France.
He finished third overall.*

2. Louison and Fausto Coppi; Paris, Autumn 1954.

3. Louison, Jean and their wives on their way back to France after the Champions Concert at the Albert Hall, November 1954. Seeing them off is Jock Wadley.

4. The first issue of Jock Wadley's monthly magazine Coureur/Sporting Cyclist *carried this portrait of Louison by Glen Steward on its cover.*

5. *Jean leading the winning break in the 1955 Paris–Nice. Brian Robinson (2nd in line) was the last to be dropped. The third rider is Roger Chupin.*

6. *Louison and Jean on the finish line.*

7. Paris–Nice 1955.

8. Signing an autograph before the start of the 1955 Tour in Le Havre.

9. *Tour de France 1955 (with Anthonin Rolland).*

10. *The early slopes of Mont Ventoux. Louison in his rainbow jersey leads with Charly Gaul (on his right shoulder).*

11. *Louison, higher up Mont Ventoux.*

12. The Bobet brothers at a post-Tour Criterium.

13. Giro d'Italia 1957: Louison regained the pink jersey in the time trial stage, but eventually lost the race to Gastone Nencini by 19 seconds.

14. Vuelta a España 1956: Louison and Jean in French national jerseys.

15.   ...and in Paris–Roubaix 1956.

16. Passing through Pleyben in Brittany on a training ride…

17. …and receiving food from their wives.

18. Jean encouraging a group of young English riders, Tour d'Ouest 1958.

*19. Jean at Herne Hill, 1962, now a journalist preparing
an article on British cycling.*

*20. Louison retires from his last Tour de France at the summit of the
Col d'Iseran. Gino Bartali looks on.*

21. Louison Bobet on the Col d'Izoard – an icon of the Tour.

22. One Sunday morning.

La volupté

People ask me whether I actually enjoy cycling. This question surprises me, since the answer is so obvious. Yes, cycling is enjoyable, and one can even give enjoyment to others, at times, but all in all it's a rather banal question.

The divine surprise comes when you discover that beyond enjoyment lies the thrill of *la volupté*. The voluptuous pleasure you get from cycling is something else. It does exist, because I have experienced it. Its magic lies in its unexpectedness, its value in its rarity. It is more than a sensation because one's emotions are involved as well as one's actions. At the risk of raising eyebrows, I would maintain that the delight of cycling is not to be found in the arena of competition. In racing the threat of failure or the excitement of success generates euphoria at best, which seems vulgar in comparison with *la volupté*.

The voluptuous pleasure that cycling can give you is delicate, intimate and ephemeral. It arrives, it takes hold of you, sweeps you up and then leaves you again. It is for you alone. It is a combination of speed and ease, force and grace. It is pure happiness.

That day – a clear, crisp February day – I was riding alone on the Côte d'Azur. Coming out of Lavandou, towards the Massif des Maures, the road leads uphill. The gradient was just right: not slowing me down too much, keeping me tuned into the hill and the chain tension in harmony with the correct gear, which selected itself automatically. My hands, resting on the handlebars, were in full control. I could see my front wheel taking on the road: black asphalt, white gravel. I felt the strength flowing from my kidneys, transferring to my thighs and down to my pedals. Either I was part of the bike, or the bike was an extension of my body, but either way the bike and I were at one. I wound up the slope to the rhythm of my breathing and perspiration: softly and smoothly. I was making headway, advancing, progressing more than I had done before. So much so that the summit of the Col de Gratteloup took me by complete surprise. The descent is so gentle that you do not stop pedalling. The gradient was just right to keep me tuned into the long plateau. Then I unwound just as I took the bends: effortlessly and fluidly. The chestnut trees flickered past on either side; the speed whistled in my ears, on the way to the Col de Babaou and then the ancient village of Collobrières, places that set you dreaming. I had everything: the image, the sound and the imagination... And then I felt thirsty and stopped for a drink. That was it, the enchantment had been broken, but 30 minutes of *volupté* is not to be sneezed at. The proof was that when I got back and Louison asked me how it had gone, I replied quite naturally: 'I was flying today.'

Another time I was with Louison, in the run-up to the Tour of Lombardy. Both of us were in shape, taut and receptive. We were feeling fed up with the rain which had been frustrating our training for two days when finally the weather brightened up late on that Friday afternoon. We decided to go for a ride. We were staying above Lake Como and, because of the humidity, we sensibly slipped down towards the lake and followed the shore for a while. Then we headed back up the narrow road which led to our hotel in Brunaute, less a village than a hamlet. Gradually the night enfolded us and, in the sweet mugginess of the air after the rain and of our perspiring bodies, we synchronised and settled into a faster tempo. Shoulder to shoulder, keeping pace exactly because we had automatically selected the same gear, we climbed the slope at a speed that amplified the darkness. Images and sounds receded, apart from the lights of a few isolated houses and the barks of a few dogs, surprised by the passing of this yoked pair. United, side by side, we were at one with the rhythm of the perpetual motion we had engaged. It was magical. But the headlamps of an enraged car woke us with a start. It was over. The magic had evaporated, but it still comes back to me now, 50 years later. I remember: we were not touching the ground; we were flying.

When I think about it, there is flight (*vol*) in *volupté*.

VIII

THE VENTOUX

July 1955. It was the time of the crowning glory, the third successive victory in the Tour de France. A sense of solemnity gradually descended on us.

Without any particular reason, Louison was anxious. The route was a classic. From the *Départ* in Le Havre it headed for the cobbles of the North, a stage in Belgium, crossed the Vosges and made a stop-over in Switzerland – the only unknown – before mounting an assault on the Alps. He reckoned the French team to be currently the best in the race. His distinguished team-mates: brother Jean, Antonin Rolland and Bernard Gauthier were joined by such talented and experienced riders as Darrigade in his capacity as French Champion, Geminiani because he was Geminiani, and Dotto, Forestier, Malléjac and Mahé.

The race was wild and unbridled, untameable. But Louison made his first mark by winning in Liège; Antonin Rolland seized the *maillot jaune* in Metz, and I occupied third place on General Classification. We thought we had effectively taken control when the situation suddenly deteriorated. Kubler led us a merry dance across Switzerland, even if Darrigade asserted himself in Zurich. The Dutch were so unruly they were driving us mad, and we faltered in the Alps. The

Luxembourg climber, Gaul, quickly baptised 'Angel of the Mountains', took off up the Galibier and, in Briançon, made up ten minutes on Louison. The newspapers laid it on thick again.

Was Bobet as strong as they said? Were his team-mates not over-stepping the mark? Was mutiny on its way? I tried to conceal or play down the unkind words and the nasty questions put to me for transmission to my big brother, who was worried, frustrated, on edge. The smile made a cautious return the next day, however, after Geminiani's timely win in Monaco.

But the malaise was palpable. Louison was becoming more and more nervous, and now he had several good reasons. The entire peloton was watching him. The attacks were coming from all sides, from every part of the bunch. Wherever it went, for more than 1,500 kilometres, the French team had felt it was being persecuted.

I was beginning to believe it myself.

On the Monaco–Marseille stage Louison threw a tantrum and decided to 'box Charly Gaul's ears' by laying waste the opposition at the feeding post in Toulon. It was carried out very effectively: the Gaul in question was declared 'weak at the knees' at the finish, having lost much of his swagger in the midsummer heat, where he was not really comfortable. At the velodrome in Marseille the French team expectantly awaited their leader's gratitude. They were disappointed. Louison had heard a few whistles from the crowd during his lap of honour. Every day, whether he won or not, he was asked to take a lap of honour in his capacity as reigning world champion. But the people of Marseille could not care less about the rainbow jersey. What they wanted was Bobet in the maillot jaune, right there, right now. After all, the Tour de France had been under way for eight days now.

I told the team that the boss was in a temper and that we'd have to wait a while for the congratulations. I knew my brother, you see. With him, it took very little to poison a moment of happiness. Just one person criticising him was enough to send him off the rails. Geminiani, who, as usual, had understood the situation, summed it up with a joke: 'Goodnight, children, it's school in the morning.'

Very early in the morning, indeed, the atmosphere was electric. Tense. There's going to be trouble I thought to myself.

There was trouble. The French team decided to do a sortie d'hôtel, that is, to attack from the off. Along an endless false flat on the motorway the peloton stretched itself out, re-formed, frayed, re-grouped, was distended once again, and finally split. There were about 20 of us in front, with Rolland, Geminiani, Mahé, Forestier, Malléjac, Louison and me from the France team. I was feeling pretty good. I knew what the little knocking feeling in my stomach was: fear before the Ventoux. For two days people had been talking about nothing else but the Ventoux. I had climbed it before, from the Malaucène side, but that was child's play, apparently. The southern ascent, from Bédoin, is terrible. And if it's hot, it turns into hell.

It's very hot. I'm going to hell. Not a word. Nothing is more impressive than a silent peloton. Nobody says a word, nobody laughs. Lifting your head slightly you can make out the shape, in the distance, through the mist, of the Ventoux.

We're riding on the rivet, and yet Ferdi Kubler somehow manages to slip through our fingers. Luckily, Geminiani goes with him. Louison comes up to see how I'm getting on: 'All right?' 'Yes,' I say. Niceties out of the way, he gives me my orders: 'With Mahé and Forestier you're going to rip to the the foot of the col. That's where it's going to explode.'

Mahé, Forestier and I are riding at the head of the group. The news isn't bad. Ahead of us, Ferdi and Gem are in range and, behind, the peloton is losing ground. Everyone around us is getting excited. The cars and motorbikes of the race followers pass us, stop, set off again. I sense that it's going to be worth giving everything. I feel that something is happening, I'm sure the race is about to tip. And I'm getting excited myself: I'm a hell of a guy, because I'm in on this decisive move. And I'm going fine.

Still, it hurts your legs this bit of descent after Carpentras. Up it goes again, up a false flat towards Bédoin, and Louison comes alongside me to whisper that he's not feeling well, not well at all. Knowing him as I do, that's a good sign. When you leave Bédoin the legs really start to hurt. François Mahé's head starts leaning a little further to the right; Jean Forestier is a little flatter over his frame. I must be listing a bit as well and the pace may be slackening. 'Two more kilometres on the rivet!' It's Louison. He's feeling a bit better, I can tell.

I'm sure I'm going to implode at the foot of the Ventoux. With 20 kilometres to climb, I'm on my knuckle ends. I'll never get used to those damn false flats before the cols. One more kilometre and I'll drop out. I can read the state of play: Ferdi and Gem, still a minute in front, the peloton two minutes away and a cloud of dust behind. Not much in return for all that effort. If I start calculating, thinking about it, it's all over. It's already all over. I'm having trouble staying ahead. Some of the hard men are catching up with me – some Belgians, some Italians. There is Louison, not looking at me, seeing nothing. I can smell gunpowder... Shit! My front tyre has gone. Well, no regrets now, that's it. In any case, I can't repair it, the mechanic is still down there, way back, in the car. Standing up, my legs are hurting even more than in the saddle. The mechano does the repair and Marcel Bidot shouts, 'Take water now, Jean. There isn't any further up.' And then, suddenly, in an instant, everything disappears into the mountain. I am still standing there, alone.

There is nothing more sinister than a disappearing peloton. You can still hear the sound of tyres on tarmac, the panting of the riders, the cries of protest between chains and dérailleurs and then, following on, the humming of motors in the caravan. Then, after the first bend, comes the silence. And here am I on the side of the road, out of it all, out of the Tour...

'And the desert becomes still again,
when the heavy travellers fade on the horizon.'

This is a fine time to be reciting poetry. Poetry doesn't push you uphill. Into the saddle. Into the desert.

This business has cost me two good minutes. Calm down now. The problem is getting to Avignon this evening. Here comes the racket: motorbikes, whistles, shouts. No point looking up, I'm back with the peloton. It's suffocating in the pack. You can smell the fear of men going to a lingering death. The road twists to the left, the famous corner, banked like for motor races. Now the going gets tough. Two or three grimpeurs, who'd go up trees like marmosets if they had to, shoot off at top speed. As if there were no slope at all. I don't have to stay with this bunch. I get over to the right and let the ones in a hurry come past. There must be a good 15 kilometres before the top. No need to panic.

I had seen it in training: a sensible 45x24, hands on top of the handlebars, chest out, cap back to front to protect the nape from the sun, eyes fixed on the road ten metres ahead and no further, whatever you do, and I get my breath back.

I drift past some of the other lads. Some not looking great, some completely knackered.

There are folk lining the road now. People with bare torsos, lucky devils, and carrying water. And they're handing it out. One with his watering can sprays me from neck to shoes and shouts to his mates: 'Water, water, he's French!' It's great to be French on a col in the Tour de France. Not so great as being Italian in a col on the Giro – there, they push you as well – but still great. I want to ask for news of the leaders, but I wouldn't hear a thing over the shouting.

Now what? The road is blocked. Or nearly. A crowd on the right, a bike on the ground, photographers, gendarmes and a quack. I saw the doctor all right, wearing shorts: it's Dr Dumas (the Tour medic). A fall? Surely not, climbing at 15kph?

Emptiness again. Not an inch of shade, nothing but bloody sun everywhere. So thirsty. Suddenly, I'm back with Jean Forestier. It looks like young Jean's a bit done-in. But he can talk: 'Did you see Malléjac?' No, I didn't see Malléjac, and besides, everybody in the team knows very well that I never see anyone, or anything. 'He's in a bad way. He's half-dead.' So that's why the doc was there on the road just now. I stay with Jean Forestier. I'm going a bit more slowly, but it's good to have some company again and we can finish the stage together. Not counting the fact that the spectators like to see two fellow-countrymen together, and there'll be more to drink.

And Jean Forestier knows everything: 'Kubler has cracked. Louison's in front with two or three Italians and Brankart, I think… You know, there are 25 blokes ahead of us at the most, no more. But there are eight kilos left to climb.' And he can talk, young Jean.

People, lots of people. Shouting: 'Bobet in the lead! Bobet's away!' There are no more trees, only people now. And Louison is putting on a virtuoso display. And this evening he'll tell us that he wasn't feeling well. And Geminiani will crack up.

Back to serious matters. Jean Forestier isn't going as fast as I am. I explain that I'll keep going at my own speed, and wait for him on the descent so we can go down to Avignon together. And I'm on my own again. All alone, that is, in the middle of all these people and their deafening roar.

Surely not? There's someone barring my way. Is he completely crazy? He's right across the road, from the cliff to the ravine, and the ravine to the cliff. And he's crying. A Belgian. I've never seen a man cry like that. He's going to fall in the ravine, I swear. I pass him, or rather cut across him. He's lost in the blackest fog. He didn't even see me.

An over-excited spectator, brandishing a bottle of water which I get ready to grab, leans over my front wheel and runs after me: 'Not for you, you bastard! Get your own!' I'm out of breath but, thank God, I manage to let fly with, 'Piss off!' Not very loud, but nice and clear. The bloke stops in his tracks, taken aback, rooted to the spot. However did I manage to find him I wonder.

Good God, it's Dad. Only two kilometres left. It must be, because yesterday evening he said: 'We'll be two kilometres from the summit.' I aim towards him, brush past him so he doesn't have to shout and so I can hear him properly. 'It's all right, old man... Louison's on his own, a minute ahead. He's fine...' I nod to show I've understood: it's less tiring that way. But it's the same old story with Dad: he never has anything to drink... Mum must be there, too, somewhere off to the side, so as not to see too much. I have to admit that it's no sight for a mother, a son – two even – on top of the Ventoux.

But who cares, mates, we're going to win the bloody Tour. We'll have to spit on our hands between here and Paris, but we're going to win it, this bloody Tour... As long as I can get through... Let me through! They've got to be crazy, these people, there's no room left on the road. A bend to the right. Christ! It's impossible. It's so hard, I'm standing still. Out of the saddle for a bit and everything hurts. I can't go on. I lift my head. I see the red kite at the summit and hear the roars, see the hands waving me on. The circus... I cross the line, unable to turn the pedals any more.

Number 2 – at 13 minutes and 15 seconds.

I loosen my toestraps.

Silence. Then, emptiness. There's nobody left. At 60kph my bike bears me towards Malaucène.*

After the finish supporters on bikes escorted me to the hotel. Noisily.

In Avignon the excitement was still at its peak People clapped me on the back: not once, but three times. One, Bobet had won the stage; two, Bobet was going to win the Tour and, three, so was the French team. At the hotel door a mechanic took hold of my bike, and had just enough time to say, 'Well done, Jean.' Back to sobriety.

At hotel reception Marcel Bidot shook my hand and said, 'Well, done, Jean' as well. Was that all, after what I had just done? That was all, except to add: 'Go and see your brother in his room. He's recuperating. He wants to see you.' Intoxicating.

The elevator and the hotel corridors were very gloomy and silent after the tumult and the sun on the Ventoux. I finally found the room and went in. The room was dark.

After a few seconds I was able to make out the bed

---

* Author's note: this account of the ascent of the Ventoux has previously figured in a book entitled *Cyclisme de plaisance* (pub. Prosport).

124

and what I thought must be a rainbow jersey. The world champion was stretched out on the bed. He was still wearing his shoes. I could not believe it, because the rider's first act, on reaching his room, is to remove his shoes. He groaned when I tried to take them off and when I tried to open the curtains: 'Don't touch anything. I'm all right like this. Listen to me.' I sat down on the edge of the bed and listened. All the same, I wondered what I was doing there in the dark, in the quiet, while in the road outside I could hear the crowd chanting, 'Bo-bet, Bo-bet!'

Louison murmured: 'Come closer. Listen. Closer.' And he mumbled, in snatches, that he was done in... he couldn't move... he was in pain, all over... he couldn't carry on... he'd lost everything... all that effort had been for nothing... the others would attack tomorrow. What was I to say? What could I do?

Overcome by the mortuary atmosphere I started whispering back. I said that I could tell him a thing or two about the others: Malléjac, who was in hospital, Kubler, who had dropped out, the Italian *directeur* who had been knocked down, about all the others, every one of them spent, hammered at the finish. And what's more, there had been about 50 still back down the road when I left for the hotel. And I assured him that they would not be queueing up to attack tomorrow.

He moaned and fulminated. He tried to turn over, in vain. He lay there, shapeless. In an even lower voice he added that most excruciating of all was his saddle sore, which he was sure had re-opened, because the pain was killing him. I could not bear it any longer. I suddenly felt the fatigue come over me. And that was when he bawled at me: 'Even you, you don't understand. Nobody does. I'm dead, completely dead.' I no longer had the strength to reply. I needed air. I left the room. In the corridor I fell, literally, on Raymond Le Bert, who gave me a shake: 'Don't worry, young Jean. We'll buck your brother up again. Now look after yourself. Quick, get in the shower.'

He was bucked up again. But I still think that, on that day, as on two or three other similar occasions, Louison gave beyond his limits.

He would maintain a strange relationship with this one mountain, the Ventoux, for the rest of his life. Whenever he was asked, again and again, to tell his Ventoux story, I would always hear him talk about his suffering, but never his joy at winning in Avignon. Every time he would say that he had been martyred that day. If it is true, as Victor Hugo says, that 'martyrdom is sublimation, a torture that consecrates', then Louison was quite right. His consecration in Avignon was, in my view, the crowning moment of his career.

Bear in mind that all riders have a strange relationship with the Ventoux, more than with any other mountain, throughout their lives. In this connection I have discovered – very late, to my great regret – the testimony of the most extraordinary champion with whom I have rubbed shoulders, without really getting to know him. In 1955 the peloton counted in its ranks an Australian named Russell Mockridge. He was a remarkable fellow. A bespectacled intellectual (sorry, but that's how it was), he was still wavering at the age of 27 between the competing vocations of cycle-racing and the priesthood. As a cyclist he had first appeared in the firmament at the 1952 Helsinki Olympics, taking two titles and therefore two gold medals in track events, outclassing the dumbfounded Europeans. That same year, and the next, he had won the Grand Prix de Paris, the celebrated sprint event, at La Cipale in Vincennes, in both the amateur and the professional categories. At the beginning of 1955 he had also taken first place at the Paris Six-Day, in the company of his compatriots, Strom and Arnold. These two rogues belonged to the *Six Jours* mafia known as the 'Blue Train', and victory in Paris had been promised to them in return for services rendered on other cycling tracks. It was only after the finish that Russell Mockridge was informed of the conspiracy. He developed such a disgust for it that he decided to give up the track and devote himself to road-racing. After promising beginnings he caught the attention of the Tour de France selectors. Signed up for a team baptised 'Luxembourg–Mixed', he found himself alongside Charly Gaul and other riders from the Grand Duchy. As these people were no playmates of ours, I had hardly followed the Australian's career.

Now, 50 kilometres from Paris, during the final stage of this difficult Tour (just 69 finished out of 130 starters), Jacques Goddet had Louison called over to his car to congratulate him and, above all – 'above all, my dear Louison' – to recommend that he savour the historic moment of his third consecutive victory. I was riding alongside Louison, spare bike *oblige* and, at the conclusion of this courtly exchange, we rejoined the peloton. Or rather, we caught up with Russell Mockridge, who had dropped back by about 20 metres, the better to enjoy the moment, which was historic for him as well. I drew alongside him and heard him singing, 'It's a long way to Prince's Park, It's a long way to go...' Up came Louison, and Russell Mockridge addressed him: 'Bravo, Mr. Bobet. It's a grand day for you! For me, too... after the Ventoux.'

I was speechless. This Olympic track rider, the antipodean phenomenon, was rejoicing at being there, at the gate of the

Parc des Princes. In his way he too had crossed the Ventoux, the Giant of Provence. Three years later Russell Mockridge was killed in a road accident during a race in his native Australia. The very first lines of his *Memoirs*, published posthumously by his wife, run as follows:

'It will be hell on the Giant today, Russell,' said my masseur, as he nursed my legs with his gentle fingers.

It seems that the call of the Ventoux can be heard as far away as Australia.

But I should still relate the *dénouement* of that Tour de France. After Avignon, all the way to Paris, Louison never once emerged from hell: for ten days and 2,000 kilometres. In the Pyrenees the re-opening of his saddle sore left him in agony and vulnerable, a fact the entire team sought to camouflage, day after day. However, when the last time trial came round, between Châtellerault and Tours, the race followers noticed that the *maillot jaune* stood up all the way, unable to sit down. Certain observers talked of a Pyrrhic victory.

Maybe so, but in Paris it was the result alone that counted. Not only was Louison Bobet declared the victor, but he was also fêted as the first man to win three consecutive Tours.

France both acclaimed and claimed him. Over the next two months he made 39 appearances in track events or criteriums. His every performance, whether in the biggest city or the smallest village, was preceded or followed by an official reception. From one day to the next we (I raced with him everywhere) went from Bourges to Abbeville, from Bruay to Creusot, from Angoulême to Belfort, from Paris to Basle, from Châteaulin to Cavaillon...

We finally set our luggage down after the Tour of

Lombardy, on 26 October. I calculated that we had clocked up 117 racing days. That was enough. Too much.

At the end of the year Louison no longer had any choice. In order to rid himself of his recurrent inflammation of the perineum, he had to undergo surgery. The operation took place with the utmost discretion, at a clinic in Dinan. It was a delicate operation, with painful consequences. The healing process demanded much care and rest. It was then, to relieve his impatience, that Louison threw himself into what was to become the other passion of his life: aviation. At the local flying club they fashioned a specially adapted pilot's seat for him, to accommodate his fragile tail-end. He obtained his first-category pilot's licence at the first attempt, with distinction and, while he was at it, his second-category licence as well. In this way he could get himself quickly across the country, from town to town, and from aerodrome to aerodrome. He bought a 'plane – a Jodel D112 – a two-seater model that enabled my promotion: I was appointed navigator. This meant that, inside the aircraft (I love the French word, *aéronef*), I occupied the right-hand seat, with the aeronautical maps spread across my knees. Louison was very quickly recognised as a fine pilot. He had the touch, and immediately picked up the three-dimensional sense required. He manoeuvred with such ease that the passengers he invited on board immediately felt reassured.

The only thing was that this fine pilot was also an imprudent one. He was qualified to fly under 'visual flight rules'. That is, he could travel whenever the meteorologist gave him authorisation. The make-or-break instinct of the champion, however, sometimes prevailed over the prudence of the pilot. It was not unknown for Louison to take off in mediocre weather, and even in weather that could only be described as bad. Once, I landed with him 'among the cows', on an extremely steeply-sloping field in the hills of the Perche region. It was quite an experience: not a particularly pleasant one, but Louison's skilful handling ensured that not too much damage was done. During this forced landing in the cowfield we had a guest on board (the new 'plane was a three-seater model by the pretty name of *Jodel Ambassadeur*). After circling two or three times to identify the best place to land, Louison pretended to our guest that we had to make an emergency landing because we had run out of fuel. Our friend did not suspect a thing, and even found the whole operation rather amusing. This passenger was a celebrity. His name was Georges Cravenne, and he was organiser of all the great artistic and high-society galas, which was why Louison's name had found its way into his address book.

Another jaunt ended up causing a stir, too. One April day we had to get to Plonéour-Lanvern, on the tip of the Finistère beyond Quimper. The 'plane seemed the perfect solution for such a trip, and we took off from Toussus-le-Noble. Somewhere around Le Mans the cloud cover became noticeably lower. Above Rennes it was about 500 metres (even if Louison announced it as 1,500 feet!) and the rain was joining in the fun. The pilot, sole master on board, decided not to land in Rennes, which boasted a sumptuous aerodrome, but to continue our journey by 'sitting on' the railway line. We flew over Redon, Vannes, Auray, Lorient at an ever-decreasing altitude, and were hopping the hedges by the time we reached Quimper. I had the map on my knees but was navigating blind, especially when, just after Quimper railway station, the line – my only reference point – disappeared into a tunnel! In the end, Louison, blessed with extraordinary eyesight, spotted the aerodrome's landing strip and managed to pull off the landing under the beating rain and the oaths of the control tower operator. The real imprudence was committed after this incident: Louison told the story to Geminiani, who re-told it, with his own embellishments as you can imagine, to his mate Fernand Raynaud, who turned it into a sketch that would have the whole country in stitches.

Later on, in the seventies, Louison passed me the controls of his thalassotherapy centre* in order to devote himself to the studies and examination leading to a professional pilot's licence. Having passed, he realised one of his life's great ambitions. On board his twin-engined Beechcraft, he crossed the Atlantic twice, together with his son who, incidentally, was a captain in a large airline company.

---

* A health centre situated on the Brittany coast based on the curative powers of sea water.

IX

THE GAP

1956 did not escape the rule governing even years. It was the worst ever, and also the most deceitful, because it began with a fanfare and ended in nightmare.

In the month of January Louison's presence was required elsewhere. The Dinan surgeon had prescribed a rest period of at least two months to allow the wound to heal properly. Raymond was so worried his champion might return to training too early that he persuaded him to take a holiday to the Canaries. I found myself alone in Issambres, but I was determined – they didn't say motivated in those days – to prove that I had mastered my subject. At the end of the month disaster struck in the form of a metereological phenomenon never seen before or since. In a single night half a metre of snow fell over the coast of the Var. The whole region was plunged into a state of emergency: without water or electricity and isolated from the mainland. It was a slap in the face for racing cyclists, condemned to inactivity for an indefinite, but certainly considerable period.

With a precise training timetable to stick to, I was not prepared to accept this fate. I learned that no snow had fallen beyond the Massif de l'Esterel, to the east of Cannes, and decided to get myself over to Menton where the roads were dry. It took three hours of driving and sliding to cover the 50 kilometres between Issambres and Cannes, and a further two hours for the last 60 kilometres to Menton. But it was worth the effort. From the very next day after my rally over snow, I took up my training programme where I had left off. The comrades who stayed in Issambres – and who had called me 'as crazy as your brother' – were forced to remain idle for ten days. In February this is a serious handicap. With superior mileage on the clock, I dominated the first races of the season and, in early March, I won the Genoa–Nice, a Côte d'Azur classic of 200 kilometres which – alas – made me the inaugural winner of the André Costes Trophy. André Costes was a journalist on the newspaper *France-Soir* who had been killed in an air crash just a week earlier, while reporting on the snowbound region. He had been a very dear friend of ours, and of Raymond Le Bert. A year later, in 1957, it was Louison – could it be a sign? – who won the second André Costes Trophy.

On his return from the Canaries Louison's tan paled by comparison with his impatience, and he was back on his bike a month earlier than expected. Despite a considerable training deficit – he reached the 1,000-kilometre mark as I was clocking up 3,500 – he found his place in the peloton again: in the tail, at first, but very soon in the middle. A month after Genoa–Nice I was no longer prancing ahead on my own: Louison was already back with me. In the Paris–Vimoutiers race, which we called the Paris–Camembert and which served as our last training session, five days before the Paris–Roubaix, we went to pieces somewhat. I was caught five hundred metres from the finish, and Louison came in only second. 'It doesn't matter,' said Raymond Le Bert, 'the main thing is that your form is there.'

Our form was certainly there – Louison won the Paris–Roubaix, the race of the cobblestones that shake you up, toss you about, rattle your teeth. In a word, the race forbidden to any man carrying a still-fresh scar in the area of you know where. The commentators talked of a miracle, and rightly so (this was the Paris-Roubaix I recounted in a previous chapter). Louison was as surprised as anyone and, in his enthusiasm, he agreed – in return for a goodly number of pesetas – to lead a French team in the Tour of Spain, which would set off a fortnight later.

In those years the *Vuelta a España* started and finished in the Basque country. The 14 stages would lead us through Madrid, Valencia and Barcelona, certainly, but in the end it was around Pamplona, San Sebastián and Vitoria that the race would be won or lost. Franco's Spain was not a thriving economy, to judge by the state of its deformed and badly-surfaced roads. Louison's tender seat did not hold up to this treatment, and the French team lost its leader at Zaragoza, after eight rather uneventful stages. The leader's brother, meanwhile, was not doing too badly. At San Sebastián, after the last time trial and four days from the finish, I was lying seventh in the general classification and fourth on points. Raymond thought this 'very good, my lad'. Little did he know that the telephone was about to ring.

A short digression is called for to explain that a rider engaged in a Grand Tour abroad cuts himself off, wittingly or not, from the events and movements of the outside world. His universe is reduced to bike, rest and sleep. The single exception, my one privilege, was that my wife – unique among the species – kept in touch every day by post. If the telephone rings during a Grand Tour, it throws you off-balance: it is inopportune, to say the very least. On 11th May 1956, when the telephone rang in Vitoria, it was utterly sickening. I was engrossed in an examination of the profile of the damned Col d'Orduña, said to be a hell of a slog, when a voice that was dear to me, but hard to recognise, started telling me about a visit from the gendarmes, the class of 52/2, and mobilization for Algeria…

A few hours later I abandoned the race on the Col d'Orduña. A few weeks after that I found myself in the nauseating hold of a troop ship bound for the other side of the Mediterranean. Across the gap.

Together with 400,000 'recalled' young people – I was older than most because my studies had deferred conscription – I was mobilised for a campaign of pacification in Algeria.

Under a bivouac on the roof of the harbour station in Algiers, I was struggling to grasp the situation. In February I had raced here in the Algiers Grand Prix, albeit limited to a city circuit because 'some people were playing the fool in the interior,' in the middle of an enthusiastic crowd. Barely three months later and here I was again, in combat uniform and a helmet. It was the beginning of a war that would never speak its name. A war that I would have trouble understanding, and will most certainly refrain from describing here.

My 'campaign' came to an end on 4 November, a date when riders hang up their bikes for another year. It was a shock to find that they had just had a season like any other. The period from May to November 1956 is a yawning gap in my cycling career. More worryingly, it also represents a gap in my memory, and I always have to make an effort to remember the names of the winners of the big races that year.

I do, however, have a more disturbing memory of 1956. Military regulations stipulated that those 'recalled' had no right to any leave during the course of their service. In the month of August, however, I was sent on a special 36-hour mission to Paris. It was on a trifling matter, but it left me greatly confused. I discovered that metropolitan France, as I had learned to call it, knew nothing about the situation in Algeria, and did not want to know. Apart from my wife, of course, my own immediate family did not listen to my current worries or my fears for what was coming. In fact, they did not ask me about it at all. Early that August what really troubled the Bobet family was the fear that 'Louison might have tonsillitis. Do you realise he could miss the world championship?'

No, I had not realised. The only thing that was clear to me was that I would never again volunteer for a mission to Paris.

This difference in outlook was to develop into a lasting split. I do not hold it against my parents, who lived just like their neighbours and like everyone else. Quite simply, I was discovering rather brutal things about life from a different angle. Even though I did not suffer personally from the events, my own life can be divided into before and after Algiers. At twenty-six years of age this dawning awareness can hardly be considered precocious. Let us say that it helped me to emerge once and for all from the shield of ignorance that protects the peloton.

No doubt I am exaggerating slightly because, to be honest, frivolity was never in my nature and I have always kept myself informed of current affairs (I remember reading François Mauriac's *Bloc-Notes* columns in *L'Express*). I was struck more by the lack of understanding among racing cyclists than by the difficulty of racing itself. It was the absence of maturity and critical discourse that complicated my life in the peloton. Conversely, the other riders quashed my doubts and concerns in no uncertain terms. When, in 1955, I had seriously questioned my future as a professional racer, asking myself whether this was really where I ought to be, or if I would do better to turn elsewhere, I was the butt of much ridicule and sarcasm. Raphaël Geminiani, among others, did not refrain from joining in. Raymond became very angry and advised me, indeed ordered me, not to think so much.

Thinking is the great danger. It is a defect: thinking is forbidden. Riders, and champions above all, are neither uncertain nor indecisive. They know only certainties. Of a dangerous, even a superior rival, they say, 'This bloke has got two legs like you and me. End of story.' Of a new rider in the peloton they either say, 'He's an idiot,' or, 'He's a good bloke'. It does not get more complicated than that.

I, however, was a difficult customer. Complicated, rational, with doubts. I recognise that this was a source of annoyance for my closest team-mates, and that it did not help me on the climbs. I strove to conceal those moments of doubt, and shared them only with my wife. No doubt it had to do with the fact that we had attended the same schools and lectures, and shared the same teachers. One day I felt I had to justify myself in front of the Latinist still slumbering within her, declaring 'Cogito, ergo sum, don't you know?'* Quick as a flash she replied, 'You don't get it. In cycling, it's cogito, ergo sunk!'

It did not settle the matter, of course, but we were at least amused.

Incidentally, there are plenty of amusing stories from that time, like the following one about Louison, early in 1956. The Parisian press was once again in turmoil, when a new daily called Le Temps de Paris came out in January. Astronomical

---

* I think, therefore I am' – the famous dictum of the C17th philosopher René Descartes. Mme Bobet's revision for racing cyclists: 'I think, therefore I'm sunk.'

sums were lent to this paper, allowing it to buy sensational exclusives. This was the conviction of the sports editor at *France-Soir*, one Gaston Bénac, who had got wind of a plot that made him all the more furious because he had not come up with the idea himself. *Le Temps de Paris* had engaged Louison Bobet for his exclusive commentaries during the next Tour de France, for five million francs (1956 francs, that is). Consequently, Gaston Bénac decreed that the name of Louison Bobet should never again feature in the headlines of his newspaper. You can imagine the dismay at the *France-Soir* editorial offices, when on Sunday 6 April, Louison won Paris–Roubaix! Dismayed or not, Gaston Bénac managed to slip surreptitiously into a subtitle that 'Louis Bobet has finally won the event'.

This anecdote amuses and comforts me at the same time. I did not think very highly of this Gaston Bénac, who dressed nattily but wrote very badly. Louison paid no attention at all to the incident. Naturally, he had signed no such contract with *Le Temps de Paris*. I would have known about it, because when the demands of the press went beyond requests for contact and ordinary interviews, at which he excelled, Louison would consult his 'complicated' brother. In the case in point, I would have dissuaded him from signing an exclusive contract with *Le Temps de Paris* or with any other paper.

I intervened – when he asked me to, of course – to spare him the mental effort and, more importantly, to save him time, because there were occasions when he really did not know which way to turn. I acted for him in this way when he received a copy of the famous Proust Questionnaire.*

---

* a questionnaire put to a series of famous people about their lives, thoughts, values etc. which appeared in *Vanity Fair*

Re-reading what I wrote then, I note that I lent Louison my immoderate passion for Hemingway. The rest of the replies were his... In the same way I explained to him how interesting it would be to accept the invitation of Paul Guth (a teacher of English, I seem to remember) when he was publishing *L'Académie Imaginaire*, with original photographs and texts on forty personalities of the era. Louison was more than a little proud to find himself in third position, in alphabetical order, between Jean-Louis Barrault and Pastor Marc Boegner.*

On my return from Algeria I felt no desire whatever to go away on holiday, apart from a short pilgrimage to Brittany. Following the obligatory visit to St-Brieuc – a few days *chez Raymond* – I understood that my six months of inactivity, half a year without touching a bike, demanded that I get back on the road immediately. I was mindful of another obligation towards my employer, Mercier. 'The hard-nosed Monsieur Edmond' had had the decency not to suspend payment of my salary during my 'leave'. Many of those I knew who had also been recalled had not been so lucky.

I was hungry to make up lost time, and thirsting for revenge. At the same time Louison had a tremendous appetite, having been on a strict diet ever since his serious operation. Both of us had a gap to fill. We left, alone – without our wives, that is – for the Côte d'Azur, where we settled into a Saint-Raphaël hotel run by some friends and frequented by Raymond, on 2 January 1957.

---

* Jean-Louis Barrault: avant-garde actor, director and mime artist. Pastor Marc Boegner: influential theologian, notable member of the French Resistance and the only Pastor to be elected into the Académie Française.

X

LORETO

You can't argue with the kilometres. After six months of complete inactivity, six months without cycling, I had trouble getting back into the swing. Quite normal, said Raymond. More worrying was the loss of my bearings.

Was it possible that in the space of just six months in 1956 the cycling world could have undergone such a metamorphosis? I no longer recognised my colleagues when I ran into them on the road. They had changed their kit, and the bikes they rode as well. Names that had resonated in my ears for so many years had entirely disappeared. No more Arliguies, Dilectas, Métropoles, Rochets, Stellas. It took me some time to adjust before I could fully accept jerseys bearing the insignia, in bold lettering, of Potin, Leroux and Saint-Raphaël, alongside the prestigious names like Alcyon or Helyett. My own jersey, in a tiny, discreet modification, bore the initials BP. Only on the shoulders, so I did not notice it too much.

Professional cycling was coming out of a deep crisis.

Confronted by motorisation (the moped and the scooter were here), everyone, from the manufacturers to the organisers, jealously guarding their dominant position, and the federations running scared that the peaceful order

141

that suited them so well could disappear. All of them had fought against the invasion of the new system which was now bringing them exactly what they all needed: money. As if to save face, the old guard had grudgingly qualified the groups that had come to their rescue as *extra-sportifs*. The distinction lasted no more than one summer. The *extra* was quickly dropped and the new sponsors quickly became part of the landscape.

This revolution was accompanied by a new order in the racing hierarchy. At the very top, the G4 of super-champions crumbled away. What with Kubler running out of time (he was 38), Koblet running out of strength, and Coppi out of luck (he had just fractured his pelvis), Bobet was left alone at the helm of the flagship. The ship was still afloat, but there were no calm waters ahead for Louison. The tone of our interviews changed, as the journalists did not hesitate – often accusingly – to bring up Louison's age (almost 32), his weariness or even his thoughts about retirement. The most disturbing visit was the one paid to us by Marcel Bidot. In Louison's absence, the poor man had been through hell in the Tour de France. At the Parc des Princes there had been cheers for the provincial winner (Roger Walkoviak), and jeers for the director of the French national team.

I confess that this drama that had split the cycling nation in two over the Tour de France had somewhat passed me by in distant Algeria. At Saint-Raphaël Raymond consoled his friend Bidot, because it seemed to him that Louison was determined to take control again. Louison confirmed this, and Marcel Bidot left us, reassured by the idea that he could count on Bobet. 'On two Bobets, like in '55,' added Raymond Le Bert, with a chuckle.

Louison got off to a flying start that season, winning the second André Costes trophy in the Genoa–Nice, as I have mentioned. Two weeks later, however, Jacques Anquetil dominated Paris–Nice. Louison clung on, nonetheless, to take fifth place. Still making my comeback, I was not dissatisfied with my tenth spot overall. It was in the run of things, as I waited to get back to peak fitness. But the press reports were out of the normal run. Everywhere you looked it was being said that Jacques Anquetil, at 23 and with all his own teeth, had become a threat to Bobet, and that Roger Rivière, just 22 and exuding class, was Bobet's heir apparent. The talent of these two lads, especially Jacques, who had made an immediate impression on me, most certainly merited the attention paid to them by the commentators. But, at the same time, a strange new tone was creeping in which painted an unflattering portrait of Bobet, who was already thoroughly established, and not only in terms of sporting success. One magazine published a piece by Antoine Blondin on 'The intimate Bobet', an article of rare perceptiveness but unfortunately illustrated by photographs of Bobet's aeroplane, Bobet's American cars and Madame Bobet's fur coats. As the only survivor of the G4, and all the more exposed for that, Bobet gradually began to irritate people.

On the road, however, Louison was telling a different story. Without actually winning, we were never far from the top positions. The only false note was struck when we made a mess of Paris–Roubaix. In rainy conditions I missed a corner on the cobbles at Tourmignies and ended up deep in a muddy ditch. For the first time Louison was not around when 'the top of the cobblestone lands on the cobblestone on top', as Antoine Blondin so neatly puts it. Antoine had come to see me at the start, accompanied by a friend. On a grey morning in Saint-Denis Antoine knew very well that you do not disturb a rider, not even somebody you know well: the prospect of 260 kilometres of torment does not put you in a party mood. He risked it, however, to bring up the vague idea of 'that book you ought to write about cycling'. Please do go on, my dear Blondin... Actually, I was thinking at that precise moment about the climb at Mons-en-Pévèle, in the rain. Antoine was clearly embarrassed, but the other one, the friend, was not. He introduced himself as Roger Nimier and launched without warning into a crazy speech to the effect: 'I am sporting director at the Gallimard stable. I train writers and bring out their books. As Antoine says, I'm going to do yours.' Antoine himself, more and more ill at ease, said nothing except: 'See you at the finish.'

At the velodrome in Roubaix Antoine did come over to meet me, but respected my silence and disappointment. I was all in, and covered in mud after finishing 38th, six minutes behind the winner. There was nothing to say. Oh yes, there was! Friend Nimier had the incredible cheek to tell me: 'We can go with the book, and we'll do it without delay.' He always claimed, afterwards, that I had agreed. As it turned out the finish of Paris–Roubaix was also the start of a new adventure on which I was unwittingly and unwillingly embarking, and which I will relate further on.

The flop of Paris–Roubaix put us only partly off our stride, Louison and me, because our programme for the season had been modified for the first time. Unlike in previous years, we were still in the warm-up phase. Our first real appointment was with the Giro d'Italia, and we needed to keep something in reserve.

A little later on, in Belgium, we held nothing back at the Weekend Ardennais: the famous weekend which gives us the Flèche Wallonne on the Saturday and on Sunday the Liège–Bastonne–Liège, a grand total of 500 kilometres over two days. In the Flèche I put my mind at ease by finishing fifth on a typical Walloon-style course in sunny, if chilly, weather. I draw attention to the weather because, by the Sunday morning, it had turned grey and the cold had set in. After 100 kilometres an icy rain began to beat down on us, and it was not long before we were swallowed up by a night of the Apocalypse. It started snowing just as a cross-wind turned us into human icicles. My glasses frosted over; nearby, a bloke was peeing on his fingers to warm them up; around me I counted fewer and fewer riders. Only a handful of the most hardened managed to drag themselves, like so many ghostly figures, all the way back to Liège. Louison was among these diehards, and everyone saluted his bravery. Contrary to appearances and innuendo, Bobet showed that he still knew how to suffer. He became Louison again, and that was important.

The Giro was just days away.

I like Italy, the Italian races, Italian riders, Italian journalists and, incidentally, though I suppose you do not see much of it from a bike, the Italian countryside. In the Giro the excitement sometimes verges on hysteria, but a foreign rider can usually stay out of the way when the tifosi surge. The Giro is a perilous race: the Italian riders, every one of them as agile as a monkey, constantly scrape you in the peloton but, at the end of the day's ride, the stage towns are a dream. The 1957 Giro, from Milan to Milan in 21 days, by way of Verona, Ferrare, Frascati, Sienna and Saint-Vincent in the Aosta Valley, looked like a tempting tourist trail.

I had to forget the tourism pretty quickly. The race got off to a blazing start. For the first four days the average speed topped 42kph. In the melée, by the evening of the second stage, Louison found himself with the pink jersey on his shoulders. It had come much earlier than planned, but the

French team, a dream team containing my favourite quintet (Bobet brothers, Raphaël Geminiani, Antonin Rolland and Pierre Barbotin), decided not to let it slip. At Verona, however, Louison landed me with a crisis: he had started thinking. At eleven o'clock in the evening he dragged me outside, saying, 'I can't sleep, and it'll do us good to walk.' Note his use of the word 'us'. As it happened I had had time to have a good look at the Verona guidebook while I was in my room, and to note that our hotel was barely 500 metres from the Casa di Giulietta. It may seem a little surreal but, in an attempt to distract my big brother, who was winning but worrying, I took him to find the Via Cappello, all the while giving him an abridged version of Romeo and Juliet's tragic story. This improvised balcony scene has always remained a secret between ourselves and Shakespeare... and I might as well confess that even he did not manage to placate Louison.

After this nervy start the race became mad, unbearable. We had to fight like fishwives to control it, to hold onto the maglia rosa and our advantage, which varied from 50 seconds to... eight seconds. And then came the Loreto stage.

I would gladly say, 'Loreto, dismal plain!' if the famous shrine to the Virgin Mary had not been planted at the very summit of a hill, and the stage-finish had not been at the foot of this shrine. I remember it well. We crossed Ancona at full-pelt in order to avoid any unforeseen problems in the town, and took a right turn onto the hill, a ramp of no more than three or four kilometres. Suddenly, my legs gave out. I lost ground, changed gear, lost sight of the leaders, and crossed the line in the tail of the peloton. One hundred metres further on, Louison was sulking, Gem was mouthing off and I was drained, bloodless. But I heard someone say that 'la maglia rosa e encora francese,' by 51 seconds, and thought 'tutto va bene'.

I was wrong. An hour later came the drama of Loreto.

Tell me why it should have been on that particular day that we had an uncomfortable hotel. It was a former monastery, where each of us had a tiny cell, far from the bathroom. Tell me why, on that precise day, I decided to take some time out after the stage. The greatest mistake of my life was to let a whole hour elapse before I headed for Raymond's massage room. There was a crush of people inside. The French journalists – there were half a dozen of them with whom we formed a colony when abroad – were reeling from what Louison had just said into one of their microphones. Out of the blue he had told them he was at the end of his tether, and he was dropping out of the Tour de France. Radio news travels fast. At seven o'clock that evening the Europe 1 station in Paris exploited the scoop, turning it into a veritable bombshell. Meanwhile, back in Loreto, the incident was closed. We tried to get some sleep, because another difficult day awaited us.

When it happened we could not understand it. It was on another stage (at Chalon-sur-Saône) in a different race (the Tour of the South-East) that the most unexpected, violent and unfair settling of scores took place. Marcel Bidot, who was following this tour in a car provided for him by L'Équipe, declared himself upset and humiliated to have learned of Bobet's withdrawal via the radio. Suddenly it was not 'Louison' any more. It was Bidot's turn to make an announcement, with uncharacteristic haste: his new French team would be built around Anquetil and Darrigade. Announcement over. Without giving anything away to Louison, I was appalled. M. Marcel Bidot, who owed his fame entirely to Louison Bobet, had judged it too degrading to pick up a telephone, or even conceivably to jump on a train, and speak to his champion in person. Three laps of honour amid the Parc des Princes applause would have been ample justification for such a small amount of effort. I am firmly of the opinion that Marcel Bidot had been manipulated by the Équipe journalist who accompanied him on every race he decided to oversee. No name made the selector's list unless he had discussed it with this journalist beforehand. Consciously or not, Bidot was always under his influence. For some unknown reason the journalist had come to hate Bobet as much as he had liked Louison in the past. He had not hesitated to do his bit, when the chance came, to shoot Bobet down.

To this personal analysis, which will anger the few survivors of this story, I will add an addendum that might reassure them of my concern to be objective. It is undeniable that Louison had made a faux pas. As his brother I secretly condemned his selfish attitude, to which I will later return. L'Équipe, the official voice of the Tour de France, had something to say, too. One article was ironic about his 'cerebral fragility', Louison having inadvertently used the expression himself. An editorial accused him of discourtesy. All these comments were justified. Louison had not spared a moment's thought for the fate of his most faithful team-mates. In his haste he had pushed the loyal servant Antonin Rolland, the eternal friend Pierre Barbotin, and Jean Bobet out of contention for the national team. Geminiani, who was on the fringes, declared himself happy to have split with Bidot.

Amid this turmoil, where there seemed to be no place for reason, I tried to retrieve the situation. I reproached Louison for failing in his duty as an employee and a business partner. It had not occurred to him for an instant that he had a duty to his employer, M. Mercier. Louison admitted publicly that, if Monsieur Mercier should require it, he would reconsider his position. But my manoeuvre fell flat, particularly as M. Mercier maintained a dignified silence. And so ended the Loreto affair.

The Giro continued, and I held on. This is the race that Louison and I would recall most often. Whenever he asked, 'Remember the Monte dei Fiori?' I would reply, 'And the Monte Bondone?' Let me tell you about it.

After Loreto Louison was living on a knife-edge. Everyone coveted his leader's position and, in the unrelenting confusion, even Antonin Rolland donned the pink jersey on one occasion. We were putting all our energy into leading the race from the front, while Charly Gaul, our most serious rival, was biding his time, having an easy ride of it in the peloton. The first warning shot came on the Sion–Varese stage, after a brief incursion into Switzerland. In the colder and ever more penetrating rain, we were climbing the interminable Simplon Pass. The surface was covered in loose chippings and I did not move a tyre's width from Louison, as there were so many punctures. My mission became trickier when, on the now-slippery descent, I was on automatic pilot, unable to see a thing through the rain on my glasses. Shortly before Varese, Gaul, excited as always by the bad weather, starting gesticulating and twitching, unable to keep still. I shared my concern with my friend Marcel Enzer, Gaul's team-mate and confidant, and the good Marcel replied: 'You know, Jean, everyone's twitchy today, and Charly gets like that more than anyone when there's a war on.' It was war as we crossed Varese. I should add the important detail that the finish was not in Varese itself, but ten kilometres further on, at Campo dei Fiori. Geminiani, who knew the lie of the land, classified this Campo not as a long, hard grind, but a short, steep climb: different, but just as fearsome. In no time the road disappeared. It had been invaded by the crowd. We threaded our way through a narrow corridor amid incessant gesticulations. It might have been quite frightening, but we did not have time, because, without warning, Charly dynamited the race. He set off up the slope at a sprint and scattered the opposition on the 15 per-cent inclines he loved so much. The damage was terrible. The man from Luxembourg grabbed the pink jersey with an advantage of one minute and seven seconds over Louison. More strangely, the Italian Nencini, at 56 seconds, was placed second. The strange ascent of Gastone Nencini demands an explanation.

Gaul was untouchable. We will not talk about him. But, behind him, Louison and Nencini were pushing hard to keep as close to him as possible. On one corner Louison lost five metres to the Italian. At the next corner he lost him from sight. Nencini had disappeared into the crowd. Standing up in his car, our technical director saw the whole thing. The spectators had grabbed Nencini, passed him from one arm to the next, and up he went like a shot. The scandal provoked such a fuss that the Giro commissaires imposed a penalty of 20 seconds, which was nothing in comparison to the gains he had made by cheating. The calculations were made and re-made: Louison remained third, 29 seconds behind the dark horse, Nencini. In the French team we had to console Louison and calm Raphaël at the same time. Big Gem was in a storming rage, furious at having been passed by riders being pushed by uncontrolled tifosi, while others were pulling him back. In a tirade which at least made us laugh, he demanded no more nor less than reimbursement from Italian social security for his pump, which he had 'broken over the head of an idiot who grabbed my saddle'.

In all the mayhem I kept quiet, because I felt a little awkward. A second explanation is required here. In this Giro d'Italia I effectively became a climber, with the blessing of Giorgio Albani. This Albani was a very good rider, but not happy on the hills. He was eagerly awaited along the route because he was reigning national champion, and therefore attired in a green, white and red jersey not so very dissimilar from my own blue, red and white one of the French team. I would also like to point out that Albani was a port'occhiali – he wore glasses. In short, in the exertion of climbing, he looked rather like Jean Bobet. So, when the tifosi grabbed hold of me and propelled me uphill, shouting 'Daï Giorgio, daï!' it was nothing to do with me. And I never protested, either. Thus, in Italy, they make a good climber out of an average one. As you can imagine, I waited until the next day before telling my mates about it. I did well to wait because, even served cold, they did not see the funny side.

Looking back at the classification sheet, and ahead at the Dolomites looming in the distance, it was difficult to believe that Gaul could lose the Giro.

But he was going to lose it, through nobody's fault but his own. He committed two errors in quick succession. On the rest-day, in Como, he proclaimed to all and sundry that he had the race in the bag, but that it would be the next day, on the summit of another peak, the Monte Bondone, that he would decide, in all his superiority, exactly how far behind to leave his rivals. It was strong language that cut us to the quick. The second mistake came on the road the next day. Charly had the imprudence to goad us even more. He had seen Louison stop to satisfy a natural need, with three or four team-mates waiting for him. So, he took a lead of fifteen, twenty metres over the peloton – I saw it, because I was there – and stopped on the right-hand side of the road, laid his bike down in the ditch, and let everyone watch as he treated himself to a comfortable pee-stop. The next instant I was present at the most devastating attack in which I had ever taken part. On my left Gem burst away with Louison on his wheel, shouting something to the effect of, 'We'll show you a pee-pee party, darling.'

It was quite a ride. This tidal wave travelled over more than 100 kilometres, at over 45kph. There were five of us on the front from the French team, raging and fuming. We did not even allow a turn to those accompanying us, the experienced Van Steenbergen who never missed a break like that, and who never came back from one, and the young freshman Baldini, who was wondering what he had let himself in for. It was a delight. Behind, Gaul found himself some convenient allies and came back to within 30 seconds before cracking violently. At the summit of Bondone, he was trailing by eight minutes. He had lost the Giro.

He vowed at once to make Bobet lose it as well. And he succeeded. When Louison attacked Nencini in the Dolomites to make up his 19 seconds, Gaul put himself gleefully and effectively at the Italian's service. And in Milan the dark horse Gastone Nencini took the Giro d'Italia with a lead of 19 seconds over Louison Bobet.* But what a race, gentlemen! For me, it was the most testing, the most overwhelming and the most stirring race of all.

With our return to France came disillusionment. Nobody could care less about our Italian campaign, and at Châteaulin in Finistère I just missed out in the French championships, after a breakaway of 200 kilometres. M. Mercier, on the finishing line, did not order me, but strongly advised me to take part in the Tour de France. I went along with him and, in so doing, created a problem because there were hardly any places left. Marcel Bidot closed his door on me, because he 'could not trust Bobet's brother'. Thank you very much, M. Bidot. I finally made the *départ* in the most modest of regional

---

* Author's comment: the dark horse Nencini was no longer a surprise when he won the 1960 Tour de France, the Tour that featured the Général de Gaulle handshake in Colombey-les-deux-Églises.

teams, the Paris-Île-de-France. On the evening of the fourth stage four riders from my team went home, eliminated for finishing outside the time-limit. There was an uncomfortable atmosphere. Curiously, though, this was the moment when I found new strength and morale, thanks to the support of a splendid team-mate named André Le Dissez, whom everyone called the 'Postman', no doubt because this former telegraphist had the wit of Jacques Tati. I accompanied Jacques Anquetil, discovering this young phenomenon for myself in the two great escapes (at Charleroi and Thonon-les-Bains) which brought him the *maillot jaune*. Not only did I accompany him, but I joined in, much to the surprise of Marcel Bidot. He told me as much. It was a little late for that!

The French team was much in evidence, partly because it was a strong one, but also because it lost any adversaries worthy of the name in the first week. The oppressive heat – people were talking about a record-breaking heatwave – had eliminated Gaul and Bahamontes, and a mass *chute* had robbed Nencini of half his team. Gastone, not such a dark horse for me, after the Giro, put on a fine show. He acted as his own *gregario*, stopping at the fountains to fill his waterbottles, and won the two finest stages, in Briançon and in Pau. Throughout the race I could not help thinking that if Louison had been there we would have seen a fine revenge for the Giro. But the great thing about sport is that 'ifs' count for nothing.

I will not elaborate on my own performance in that Tour, though I regard it as the best of my career. Racing as an individual I finished in Paris in 15th place. Jacques Goddet offered his congratulations and, as in 1955, asked me to write the story of the race for his newspaper. My articles caused a certain stir. I gave myself over to a lengthy eulogy of Jacques

Anquetil, victor on his first Tour at just 23 years of age. Louison was surprised, even shocked. He as good as called me a traitor. Too bad. After all, who but Louison himself, in Loreto, had opened the way for Jacques the lad in Paris?

The end of the season was insipid. I joined the starting-lines with neither energy nor ambition. I had been drained by 50 days of racing at the front. Riding in such circumstances, without the least role to play, was unbearable. I was as depressed at the back of the race as I had been exultant at the front. At the back, moreover, I hardly saw anything of Louison, who was firmly back in the saddle and back on form. At the world championship – where Marcel Bidot selected him after all – he finished second, behind the inexhaustible Van Steenbergen. A good result. In the Paris–Tours he came in second again behind another Belgian, Fred de Bruyne. A worrying result.

For my part, I called a halt to the season at Tours. I had no legs left. My wife announced a happy event. Roger Nimier sent me a contract.

As for cycling…

Doping

If I fail to mention it I will be criticised. I will talk about it, then, despite my conviction that all the testimonies on this touchy subject are ultimately useless. Mine is based only on my own experience. The best work I have read on doping is by Professor Patrick Laure of the University of Nancy. His first chapter begins with this quotation, counselling prudence: 'Examine your words well, and you will find that even when you have no motive to be false, it is a very hard thing to say the exact truth' (George Eliot). However, I'll have a go.

My first reaction was surprise. On my return from Budapest people spoke less about my victory than about the considerable margin – over five minutes – with which I had won it. First one, then another, then ten old hands asked me the same question, in a malicious tone that I could not miss, but whose meaning I did not grasp: 'How many chemists were there in your student team?' Please believe me when I say I was completely naïve. It was only half a dozen years later that I learned that there were indeed some students who ran on Maxiton during the exam periods.

Then came amusement. Right at the beginning of the 50s, the word 'doping' meant the accusing finger, the periodic crack of the whip, so sudden and violent that it singled out the cheat in an instant. A doped cyclist was unable to control himself. His agitation, which could be dangerous, was betrayed by unpredictable riding or improbable tics, and frankly made us laugh. Louison, with his keen powers of observation, once called on me as a witness: 'Look carefully at De Rijcke. His ears are moving in every direction.' And it really was comical to see the ears of this famous rabbit twitching before he bolted. The sight ceased to amuse me in 1956 when I saw those ears pass under my nose 100 metres from the finish of the Milan–San Remo. But I repeat that, while doping was not exactly rare, it only occurred periodically. It had comical side-effects and was ineffective in its results. That was a time when it fuelled stories more than anything else. The well-known one about Roger Hassenforder feeding pills to his goldfish, in order to compare the effects of Maxiton and Tonedron, had the peloton roaring with laughter. The less well-known story about the same man tipping everything and anything into an opponent's water bottle put an end to the amusement.

Then came astonishment. Crossing the Apennines from Pescara to Naples during the 1957 Giro, we (the French team, as you will recall) needed to be vigilant, because Louison was wearing the *maglia rosa*. In the middle of about ten escapees, who did not pose much danger in the classification, Antonin Rolland and I were happy to cross the Valico del Macerone, which was said to be a trap, at the head of the race. Hardly had we begun the descent when a meteor overtook us at such a speed that no-one could follow him. The meteor himself was the first to be surprised when he turned his head. He slowed down, said something that I did not catch, let go of his handlebars, took a box from his jersey pocket, and at 50kph started handing out little tablets to everybody who wanted one. Sober as ever, Antonin Rolland warned me: 'It's serious. That bloke is Nencini. We'll stop and wait for Louison, but there's going to be trouble.' We did indeed have trouble catching that group. One week later, in the same race, we heard Charly Gaul, freshly stripped of the pink jersey and beside himself, completely out of his mind, demanding a butcher's knife so he could sort Bobet out!

Then, it was terror, and disgust. I began to notice, or guess, or suspect doping on all sides. But I refused to accept it. I could not resign myself, if I was ranked 50th, to suddenly being overtaken by the rider 70th, or even 110th. Blokes who were inferior to me (in the saddle you get their exact measure) were suddenly leaving me standing.

Adieu, then, to all that. At the age of 28 I decided to pack it in. But not without trying it for myself...

At daybreak on Sunday 5 October 1958 I met Louison at his house as usual, before heading for the start. The race was the Paris–Tours, the last one of the season, and Louison knew of my intention to quit. In a detached tone I told him that I wanted to try an experiment with the best stuff available, which boasted an unrivalled reputation at that time. The stuff was called Metedrine, and the name had surprised me when I was first offered it. I had previously read that this amphetamine had won the Battle of Britain by boosting the wellbeing and effectiveness of the pilots of the RAF. The other thing that surprised me was the offhand way the supplier gave me the stuff. I do say 'gave', because he seemed to consider dealing this bomb too trifling to be worth money to him. Perhaps he also saw it as providing a sweetener for a new customer.

The stuff could be swallowed or injected. Since I had a horror of injections I chose the former method, and split the dose in two. One for me, the other for Louison, the better to appreciate its comparative effects. That Sunday, between Paris and Tours, I soared through an artificial paradise. I saw my friends' tyres go flat *before* they noticed the punctures themselves. I went to have a word with my *directeur sportif* behind, and came straight back up to the head of the race, passing the whole of the peloton in review. I could not feel the pedals. Were they really still there? At the finish there were a good 100 of us together and this formation, quite common in the Paris-Tours, would make me one of sixty placed equal, just another rider who failed to enter the turmoil of a bunch sprint. That Sunday in October though, 200 metres from the line, I was elbow to elbow with the first fifteen. The two blokes in front of me did not seem to be going very fast, so I got ready to pass between them... and found myself on my arse in the road. There had been no space between them at all!

A fitting conclusion to my one and only escapade as a willing cheat. And the best was yet to come. When I found Louison in the shower he held out his half-portion, saying: 'I didn't take your stuff.' I felt no after-effects of tiredness or weakness in the following days. But it gave me a scare when I realised that the stuff really had made me take the climbs for descents, as my supplier had promised.

And so, farewell. Farewell to cycling, which was no longer to my taste. At 28 it was a decision that hurt, but I am neither going to play the victim nor the hero. I was lucky enough to be able to take another path. The day after my last race I was offered a new job. At the invitation of Jacques Goddet, proprietor of L'Équipe, I became a journalist. This privilege left me forgiving. Ever since then, though I do not condone their actions, I have been able to understand all those professionals for whom cycling is the only trade they know. And who, confronted with the dilemma 'to take it or not to take it?' end up taking it because 'it goes with the job'.

For all that, doping still pursued me after I left the peloton. At first I was disconcerted to discover that the journalists knew exactly what was going on. They spoke about it between themselves to show that they were not taken in, but – as we would say nowadays – they refused to communicate it to the public. Why? For a multitude of reasons which do not necessarily dishonour the profession. Some considered it pointless to denounce a practice so ancient as to be in the nature of things. Others did not have the heart to destroy the sport they loved. The majority of sports reporters in the 50s had not had any professional training. Recruited on the job, they were often former (small-time) riders themselves, or perhaps had spent their youth surrounded by cycle-racing, or bathed in regional glory. For them, cycling represented something sacred; in any case, investigative journalism had not yet been invented.

Last, but not least, I would say that the explanation for the silence of those who were best informed is more delicate. They were on such intimate terms with the riders that they were not prepared to break them. Thus they accepted a degree of complicity. This *omerta* was illustrated by the bond of friendship that united the greatest of champions, Jacques Anquetil, with the most renowned of cycling correspondents, Pierre Chany. Incidentally, I do not believe that the readers and listeners of sports journalism were yet at the stage where they craved this kind of information. In 1959 I told the story of my Paris–Tours jaunt in the *L'Équipe*'s monthly review, *Sport et Vie*. My account provoked no comment or debate. On the other hand, when I wrote two articles on the subject for *Le Monde* I was surprised to receive, through the newspaper, a letter from André Missoffe, the Minister of Sport, who wished to see me immediately to discuss the problem. He moved to another Ministry shortly afterwards.

As a journalist and a witness – some might say a privileged one – people could scarcely have confided in me more. Roger Rivière, for instance, opening his suitcase to show me his supply of Palfium. Or Tom Simpson, on the morning of his fatal climb on the Ventoux, sticking his tongue out to let me count the little white tablets he had just emptied onto it 'just to keep me going, for the start'. Those two, Tom and Roger, were just kids, totally immature. But when, in a scandal sheet, Jacques Anquetil, for all his intelligence and sense of responsibility, started to air his drug-taking, 'which only fools and hypocrites claimed to refuse,' I lost what remained of my illusions.

I set off for pastures new, to join Louison in the field of thalassotherapy. The distant echoes that reached our ears became more horrifying with every passing year. They told of medical doping, where, in effect, doctors contested the races and set the records – instead of the riders. And then doping followed the timeline of scientific progress, from the age of chemistry to that of biochemistry, and into the age of genetics. We can only wait for the age of symbiosis to begin.

Scandals turned troublemakers into stars; nauseating books sold in insane numbers; the whole culture of cycling was in the dock. Until that is, the finger was pointed at the culture of every sport: football, rugby, athletics, skiing… until the day when people started to recognise that it was Culture with a capital C that had engendered the phenomenon in the first place. For my part I share Patrick Laure's conclusion: 'History suggests that the philosophy of doping is as old as man himself who, having been given the power of thought, has never been able to accept his physical or mental limits.'

It may be a lost cause to combat something that is a natural propensity. However, it has to be done. I am still trying.

XI

LAST EMBERS

It was a strange autumn.

The day after Paris–Tours I worked out that I only had 80 days to write the book promised to Roger Nimier and Antoine Blondin. In January 1958 I handed in the 250 pages of my manuscript.* I am still impressed by my own performance: not the literary merit, but the speed.

In this project I was supported, in his own way, by the sporting director of the Gallimard publishing house, whose style was a world away from the down-to-earth sporting director of Mercier Cycles. Suddenly, I had to start reading between the lines. For one thing Nimier wrote to me.

I quote:

'I am sending you a cheque dated 1957, as you request. I have experienced a little trouble having it made out in the absence of the Gallimard family (which can be most useful for signing purposes).' And, further on: 'The book you are writing risks being less public than a biographical novel. It will also be a good deal more intelligent.'

---

* The book would be entitled *Louison Bobet, une vélobiographie*.

Nimier sometimes invited me over to his office on the Rue Sébastien-Bottin. Each time I crossed the threshold of this illustrious building I panicked at the thought of running into the eminent writers of Gallimard's *Nouvelle Revue Française*. Nimier himself rambled, came to the point, then produced total surprises. The man was a fencer, and a very fine one at that. I had never seen so much wit and perceptiveness combined in one man. Neither had I met such an *agent provocateur* or such a dissembler. He disturbed and fascinated me in equal measure. The better to understand this rare animal, I hunted him down in his books, and thought I might have been given a pointer by his lead character, the dreadful Sanders: 'We live in a poisoned age where friendship arouses sarcasm.' I was disconcerted by the elegant Nimier's bitter smile.

He also invited me to dinner once, perhaps because he was feeling the poison more than usual. At such times he would fill a table with guests, preferably in a fine and expensive restaurant, to keep himself amused. We played 'Tour de France'. Blondin played Louison. I played me. The wine waiter was always called Gregario. Paul Guimard wanted to be Geminiani, as did Nimier, and a huge argument ensued. I suggested to Nimier that he play Koblet instead. The rôle of the gifted, nonchalant charmer suited him. He was superb in the rôle. Later on I would be deeply touched, but not altogether surprised, when both Nimier and Koblet, born in the same year, disappeared within two years of each other at the wheel of their cars, at the end of a road they considered a cul-de-sac.

The cycling world was going through a strange, restless period. Thus we abandoned the classic Paris–Nice for the brand-new Tour of Sardinia, for the simple reason that the Italian organiser had the money which the French organiser

162

severely lacked. The Italian took the liberty of forming a team of five Frenchmen which, though it did not bear the label France, did bring together Bobet and Geminiani who officially belonged to two different trade-teams. His money soon ironed out any problems. It would have been bad form for me to play the difficult customer, since this was my favourite line-up, my *belle équipe*. Around Bobet and Geminiani it reunited Antonin Rolland, Pierre Barbotin, me and Raymond Le Bert. Or, as 'my' team was more commonly known, Louison and Gem, 'Tonin and Pierrot with Raymond Le Bert. At the start in Rome I was so happy that I dragged the whole troupe to the Coliseum for a photo. How strange that I should have been moved to fix this moment for posterity, as if I had a presentiment that it would be so fleeting.

The race left us with some warm memories, but also icy ones. The Italian riders had not forgotten the French rampage on the Bondone in 1957, and did not let more than a wheel's width come between us. Perhaps we would manage to find the strategy that had eluded us the previous year at Loreto. Louison did indeed make compromises, and it was Antonin Rolland, riding behind him all the way, who won when the race came to an end… before the finish. On the final stage, above Sassari, we were caught in such a violent snowstorm that the deep-frozen riders panicked and abandoned their bikes, taking refuge in the cars. The race was stopped and the previous day's rankings validated and proclaimed as the general classification. My *belle équipe* had won the Giro della Sardegna.

Once back in France, because I was trying to do too many things, I started to lose my grip. A professional athlete cannot afford to step back, even psychologically, from his sport. A rider who strays from his well-worn, sheltered road is lost. I got lost.

The adventure of the book, written during the winter break, had worn me out – sucked me dry even. Another adventure was going to prove even more exhausting.

All these years later I can no longer put my finger on all the reasons for the riders' discontent with the cycling authorities. It comes back to me now, that the Federation had a standing committee for professionals, nicknamed 'the miracle workers', but it was rarely consulted and no longer fully functioning. I also remember that one of the main grumbles was about the institutions dragging their feet over the introduction of new patrons, from outside the cycle industry. The bad feeling was all the more intense because the President of the French Federation, Achille Joinard, was also President of the International Cycling Union. Nowadays one would say it was just the moment to pile on the pressure. An impromptu meeting on the Côte d'Azur had brought together a good number of cyclists, including those with the highest profile, and let it be known that: (a) it was necessary to establish a trade union, and that (b) it was up to you, Jean, to set it up it for us. I did not refuse, because this seemed a commendable and achievable goal.

As Secretary-General (Designate), I had Louison Bobet unanimously elected President, Jacques Anquetil and Raphaël Geminiani as Vice-Presidents, and André Darrigade, Jean Forestier and a few others to various other posts, making for quite a company. I was fortunate to have such a cultivated and intelligent man as Achille Joinard on the other side of the table. In order for us to exist officially, I needed his blessing (in the world outside, M. Joinard dealt in religious artefacts). It was he that suggested we find a nuanced name for the new body, because 'the word *syndicat* [trade union] strikes fear into people.' So it was that I announced to the State authorities the birth of the Union of Professional French Cyclists

(UCPF). Very early on I was reproached for not moving quickly enough. My dear colleagues, who proved extremely difficult to bring together for annual general meetings, were not aware that, quite apart from etiquette, we also needed a constitution. I organised this with the help of a legal and tax adviser, who was paid with the first membership dues (not a great deal, in other words). I found the process quite amusing. M. Bertrand, our consultant, simply used a text he had drawn up for the professional jockeys who were, to my knowledge, the first sportsmen to have become unionised. A few months later, a player at Saint-Étienne, Eugène N'Jo Léa, would pay me a visit, to create a footballers' association with the same constitution.

Not all my memories of involvement in the UCPF are positive ones. The task knocked me off course, taking me away from my cycling career. Over trivial matters riders would accost me in the peloton to tell me – at forty kilometres an hour, can you imagine – that 'it'll all just be a waste of time and money.' More serious was our brush with the Ministry of Finance. One day I received notification to attend an official department popularly known as 'the taxman', whose headquarters, the Place Saint-Sulpice in Paris, was cursed like that of the Inquisition in the Middle Ages.

M. Bertrand came along with me and, as a man of the profession, took our warm reception in his stride. I listened complacently as an official congratulated us for representing such a well-organised body. So well-organised, indeed, that... Wham!... we should discuss one or two serious problems. The taxman's problem, on that particular day, was that while certain racing cyclists enjoyed a prominent position in the sports pages, they were missing from his records because they had never paid a centime of income tax. A number of dossiers were arranged very visibly on the table in front of us, and I was astounded to read names that I would never have imagined could be in the dock on such charges. We very prudently requested an adjournment. After two or three further meetings we managed to reach a satisfactory compromise: the authorities would make us a present of two years (or perhaps three, I do not remember exactly) out of the five that were subject to enquiry for undeclared income. I do remember very clearly indeed, however, the abuse I received from two or three riders in the peloton, who threatened to 'kick my head in if I didn't stop my bloody meddling'.

Antonin Magne, my *directeur sportif*, was doubly irritated. He was not overly pleased with the deterioration in my performance, and saw my activities as a lost cause. Though the context was different, Antonin Magne had, in his day, stirred up a huge storm when he seemed to contest the authority of Henri Desgrange, boss of *L'Auto* and of the Tour de France. In 1936 he had looked favourably on the development of the left-wing political alliance, the Popular Front. World Champion or not, he subsequently found that contracts at the Vélodrome d'Hiver and the Parc des Princes were very hard to come by. M. Magne advised me to pedal softly. 'You are wasting your time,' he told me.

From my short experience I learned that corporatism in sport has its limits, because sport always ultimately comes down to rivalry. Within a club or team, of course, co-operation, dedication to the cause and even self-sacrifice are common currency. But solidarity is always undermined by rivalry as soon as discussion turns to general principles. It has no place when the overriding principle is 'every man for himself'. Sporting unions can only set themselves social or charitable aims. This is important and long-term work, however, because there are many sportsmen in need of assistance. Unionism in sport remains the preserve of non-governmental organisations and, these days, it is an honourable calling to belong to an NGO.

In the spring of 1958 I was not the only one losing his grip. So too was Louison, although he would not admit it. That was not all he would lose.

He lost Raymond Le Bert, who decided in April to put an end to their collaboration. I was not present at the scene of their parting, which I had sensed was on its way. There had been no raised voices or unpleasant words. Quite simply, both of them had had enough, worn out by unremitting hard work which owed its success to their close co-operation, a kind of communion. The price to pay, for both of them, had been self-effacement, or self-abnegation, in order never to jeopardise the harmony between them. With the passing of the years this tacit agreement had become an onerous chore for both of them. I think it was most likely Louison who could no longer stomach all Raymond's advice.

Immediately after this parting of the ways Raymond Le Bert came to see me to say that 'Louison is too much of a big boy, now, to listen.' That is, to listen to Raymond, who was convinced that, at the age of thirty-three, an athlete who has given his all should start slowing down, choose fewer objectives, and revise his ambitions. This was just the kind of talk that Louison could not accept. On the contrary, he had decided to line up once again for both the Giro d'Italia and the Tour de France. So, Raymond took his leave, after eight years together: eight times three hundred days they had shared, for better and for worse. It hit me hard.

Louison put on a brave face. In order to replace the irreplaceable, he enlisted the services of two *soigneurs*, because it was impossible to find a single man available full-time. If I can put it this way, he found one *soigneur* for weekdays and another for Sundays. The former was an old masseur, with a calm and affable exterior. His name, Armand Poupard (meaning 'chubby-cheeks') suited him down to the ground. However, this native of Bordeaux, who had once been *soigneur* to Antonin Magne, was no longer of an age to confront the Grand Tours. The 'Sunday soigneur', for the big campaigns, was a different fish altogether. This was Jean-Paul Sereni, who ran a massage and physiotherapy clinic near the Gare Saint-Lazare in Paris. His distinguishing feature was that he was masseur to the Paris Opera. His fine manners and natural refinement looked like being a handicap when he entered the coarser world of cycling, but that was quickly overcome. Jean-Paul Sereni's great merit, aside from his professional expertise, was that he served both the cycling champion, Louison Bobet, and the prima ballerina, Claude Bessy. He first joined us on the road for the Giro. But before we set off there is something I should tell you.

In the difficult period we were going through that year, I added to the confusion. The sporting director of Éditions Gallimard brought out my book – *Louison Bobet, une vélobiographie* – and explained that there would have to be 'a signing' to mark its publication. I did not really know what this entailed, but it did not matter: the editor would arrange everything.

This was another piece of mischief on the part of Roger Nimier. The signing took place at the foot of the main staircase at the Galeries Lafayette. It was both a grandiose and a completely mad occasion. I was very grateful to Louison, who had so many demands on his time, for agreeing to take part in the ceremony, which took place in the late afternoon. There was a terrible crush on his arrival. We were on the brink of a riot. People fought to get the champion's signature, which happened to be on his brother's book. Louison, on my left, had trouble keeping up with the flow of his admirers. I would have been delighted at this success if, on my other side, there had not been standing another writer, whose latest book was being published on the same day.

Roger Nimier had had the bold idea, or the impertinence, to involve another literary figure in the signing ceremony: a proper writer, from the celebrated Gallimard collection. The Bobets' popular clientele scarcely paid any attention at all to this author, who was dedicating one volume for every twenty or thirty that we churned out. It was most embarrassing. But when I turned to the right, I beheld the embodiment of Class and Charm, with capital Cs. This writer was Louise de Vilmorin, and her book was entitled *La Lettre dans un taxi*. She showed no resentment, no frustration at all. In fact, she savoured the unconventional situation to the full. When Louison, who was seated, said 'Excusez-moi, madame...' she replied: 'Please, Louison, call me Louise.' Roger Nimier was proud of his coup: 'I wanted you to be present, my dear Louise, at the Bobets' victory in the Grand Prix des Galeries Lafayette.' These deliciously accomplished accomplices found everything highly amusing.

We were not so amused by the 1958 Giro. Louison was firmly at the head of the race and his team following, with the exception of brother Jean, who was completely off the pace. Afflicted by recurrent nosebleeds, I would often finish the stage just in front of the ambulance and the race doctor. Before abandoning the race half-way through, not far from Rome, I did at least manage to do something worthwhile. Marcel Bidot paid us a visit, no doubt in order to avoid a second Loreto. He announced rather abruptly to Louison that he was selecting the same Tour de France team as the previous year, around Anquetil and Darrigade, adding: 'I have kept two places, one for you and one for your brother.' Voices were raised, Louison considering himself mistreated, and Bidot wanting to keep all the promises he had made. I suggested a truce, so that each could retire to his tent, the better to continue the discussion in the morning. I kept Marcel Bidot back to tell him that I was too run-down to accept a place in his team. The next day Louison gave his agreement.

Without any derring-do or stage wins (for the first time in a Grand Tour), Louison nonetheless came fourth in the Giro, which was won by the young Ercole Baldini. Louison was the first Frenchman, Geminiani finishing in eighth place. He was again the top French rider at the world championship, held in Reims that August. He was runner-up, once again behind Ercole Baldini. This was an honourable balance sheet, especially if you take into account his seventh place – but first of Marcel Bidot's team – in the Tour de France. At the end of the season, during which Jacques Anquetil had marked time, Louison still cut an imposing figure. One day, however, he confided to me: 'I'm not feeling so red-blooded these days, you know.'

It was at his insistence, and Antonin Magne's, that I got back on the road in 1959. And I opened the season with victory in the Lodève Tournament. This was a 'fun' race, a fundraiser to replenish the empty coffers of the UCPF. All the riders took part on a voluntary basis and, at the end of the event, they kindly opened the door for me – for services rendered, they said – and I won the tournament. The rest of the season was rather less glorious. I went along for the ride, no more. I accompanied Louison on a new kind of Grand Prix in Italy, with an original format. Each of the eight stages (from 29 April to 7 May) consisted of two sections, seamlessly joined in the middle. After a normal race over 150 kilometres, the last 50 or 60 were ridden behind scooters (the scooter brand was the event's sole and generous sponsor). Each rider had the use of a pace-man and the race turned into an infernal racket, as speeds reached 60kph. Louison, who had insisted on having his own personal pacer, an expert named Lorenzetti, excelled at this game. Not only did he top the general classification of the race, which was also called the Rome–Naples–Palermo, but he also won five of its eight stages. The whole of southern Italy, long-deprived of big international events, was at fever pitch. This 'other' Italy acclaimed Louison Bobet and carried him off in triumph. The fanatical reception at Cosenza gave us a real scare. Swamped by *tifosi*, Louison had to be escorted to his hotel under police protection. We found his bike and the good Armand Poupard an hour later, down at the police station. The organiser was also becoming concerned. In order to pre-empt an even worse scrum at the finish of the final stage in Palermo, he moved the line to the quayside, just opposite the gangplank of the ship that would take us to Naples. From the safety of the ship's deck, Louison saluted a frenzied crowd that chanted his name until anchor was weighed.

It really was an unusual sight.

The Italian race served as a dry run for the season's principal objective. At the turn of the year Louison had agreed with Antonin Magne that he would have a go at one of cycling's monuments, the mythical Bordeaux–Paris race. It was an event that owed its prestige to its longevity (since 1902) and its originality. Six hundred kilometres in length, the race switched halfway, at Châtellerault, to a contest behind Dernys. The midnight *départ*, the long hours in the saddle lit only by the headlamps of the cars behind, the sudden burst of speed in the Loire Valley, the perilous crossing of the Chevreuse Valley, and the Parc des Princes finish had all gone into constructing the Bordeaux–Paris legend. It was known as the 'Derby of the Road', and also as the 'race that kills', because this 16-hour epic had seen some of the most horrific crashes in cycling history.

Louison prepared himself meticulously, and won the event in grand style. The Chevreuse Valley was teeming with people as he gave his masterclass on every hill, and the Parc des Princes was full to bursting when he crossed the finishing line, eight minutes ahead of his nearest rival. Though he did not yet know it, this was to be his last triumph, his apotheosis.

It was a wonderful day for Louison. Alone on the road, far ahead of the rest, he had an opportunity to appreciate, much more than at the Tour de France finishes, the tributes of a Parisian public that formed a guard of honour and chanted his name over more than a hundred kilometres. For me, there was nothing left after the 1959 Bordeaux–Paris. It was the moment I decided to draw a line under my racing career, which had lost its purpose. I did start the Tour de France, but this time as a journalist. My bosses at *L'Équipe* were kind enough to put me in the same room as an uncommonly fine team-mate – Antoine Blondin, who welcomed me in his first chronicle of that Tour:

You discover that you are to share a room with Jean Bobet, and virtually his bed. You incline your head, to look more like a racing cyclist.

The last time you saw Jean Bobet with his feet up was in Thonon, two years ago. He was running fourth in the general classification and the experts bustled around him, wielding spirometers and cardiograms...

Now, the radiators are no longer laden with cycling jerseys, but with reams of paper. And we are the ones drying up. You scrutinise your friend for some sign of the vocation he was following until just a few days ago. None comes to light. The rapid metamorphosis is complete... You smile at your nostalgic, vain attempt to track down the man of yesterday in the man of today. You resolve not to try again, but to acknowledge the transformation, and recognise that certain memories must share the fate of yesterday's bouquet, whose flowers are resigned to the loss of their pedals forever.

As I set out into journalism I immediately discovered that it was just as hard to write behind Blondin as to ride behind Coppi.

The first death

That's how it goes.

One day, powerless to prevent it, he sees the rear wheel of the rider immediately in front slip away from him. He strains his sinews. Other people cannot see it yet. He sticks at it tenaciously, but the wheel has gone, for good. To diguise his weakness he pretends to look back, he has a mouthful of water. But he knows he has become impotent.

Another day he sees the sudden, incisive acceleration of a frisky young rival. He hesitates, unable to pounce onto the young buck's wheel. He no longer feels in his muscles the elasticity he needs for a spurt. To compensate for his handicap he pedals harder and faster. But he knows he can't do it.

He no longer takes those wheels, he no longer jumps in. It's over: he will not win again. He is finished, not yet even thirty-five. Thirty-two, thirty-three, thirty-four, thirty five... The champion counts the steady waning of his powers. Thirty-two, thirty-three, thirty-four, thirty five... tolls the knell. *Too soon, the athlete feels death is upon him.*[*]

In 1959 Louison was thirty-four. I was no longer at his side, in the saddle, in the peloton. I was riding further behind, generally on a motorbike, in my new capacity as journalist

---

[*] Jean Prévost, *Plaisirs des sports*, Gallimard, 1925, La Table Ronde, 2003

and race-follower. In the Tour de France, which he wanted to tackle after Bordeaux–Paris, he suddenly realised that his courage and experience would not be enough to give him a leading role. He followed, suffered, and finally was unable to continue. The eighteenth stage, leading from Grenoble to Aosta, was so long that the start was brought forward to the summit of the Col du Lauteret. It was 14 July, but up at 2,000 metres there was no party atmosphere. It was cold and raining. I looked around for Louison and was staggered to see him in conversation with a genial looking Charly Gaul. It was more than a sign. Louison was no longer feared, but pitied. As I approached he shot me a meaningful look: there was no point talking.

Immediately dropped at the start, on the ascent of the Galibier, he came back on the way down and into the Maurienne valley, until the start of the 33-kilometre climb up to the Col de l'Iseran, 2,770 metres above sea-level. At the foot of the climb I picked out my Louison. It looked as if he was asphyxiating, desperately gasping for air. The road kept rising and I saw Louison sink still further. I could not stand it. I took myself off to the front of the race. Colleagues gave me contradictory updates: 'He's looking better'... 'He's going really badly...' I stopped halfway up the pass, between two chalets on the edge of Bonneval. Each minute I waited seemed to last an hour, until Louison finally arrived and I was able to observe him from my hiding place. I wondered what on earth was keeping him going forward and, at the same time, what could possibly stop him. I caught up with him on my motorbike, close enough to touch him. He signalled to me to go away with the unbearable, despairing look of a drowning man.

I left, as he had requested. It would not help for him to see my own distress. Further on I would learn that he had abandoned the race, *after* the summit of the Iseran. So that was what had been pulling him on, preventing him from stopping. He knew he was going to die, but he would die at the top. Everybody hailed the grandeur of his farewell to arms, in the highest of high places.

His inexorable decline could be read in his results as well as his muscles. The Bordeaux–Paris triumph was the exception, in an exceptional race. Since 1958 Louison had often been placed. With fourth, third and even a good number of second places, people hailed his consistency. But he never won any of the major races. In those, he was no longer to be seen winning. For a champion it is unbearable not to be first, because the champion knows no half-measures. It is victory or failure. And failure is inadmissible, even for a champion approaching the age limit, for the simple reason that he is still a man in his prime. He is as yet untouched by wisdom, that comes just in time, as Julien Gracq says, to the aid of the genuinely old: 'The interesting thing about old age is that desire adjusts itself miraculously to suit the means. One begins to experience only those desires that have a chance of being satisfied in the new circumstances.' The athlete, however, rejects such ignominious restrictions. At only 35, even on the decline, he still feels the desires that new circumstances deny him. He digs in his heels. In vain. And the champion is struck down by an age attack, his heart as strong as ever.

Very few people have successfully described the tragedy of a champion's foretold death, since the exercise requires not only talent, but also sensitivity and experience. I know of two writers who have done this to perfection, and am moved to quote them.

First, Alain Gerber:

It is written in the most terrible of all the laws of sport: whoever you are, you will always lose in the end. There is nothing that champions win for themselves – by bravery, sacrifice and pain – that will not, in a short space of time, be taken away. They are empty-handed conquerors. Scarcely have they reached their promised land, when they find themselves exiled once again...

Glory and fortune can be won and lost. After all, these are but worldly goods, just things. But the champion loses his title as champion. His farewell to arms is a farewell to himself.

A first death, in a sense. But what are we to think of Jean Prévost (1901-1945), who dissects and analyses the premature death of the athlete with a strange lucidity? I say strange, because this writer of genius was not yet 24 when he turned his gaze to the subject:

Death is acting on us all, every moment, but the common run of people, not much concerned with their bodies, are only aware of it at distant intervals: at times of great disaster. They are often astonished when death comes to them.

The athlete, more sensitive and finely attuned to his body, feels it quietly sapping his life-force, and anxiously counts each season's declining yield. It slips first into his feet and knees, like hemlock. Never again will they be heated by the surge of pure speed. Then his strength, which had brought him still further glory, drains away and its source clouds over. And yet the outward appearance remains splendid in what we pathetically call the prime of his life...

When his body gives up, an athlete, like an animal, is condemned to death. The end of the champion is as tragic as that of the lion king.

XII

TOMORROW, WE RIDE

On 2 January 1960, Fausto Coppi died.

It was the end of a generation of racing cyclists: that of the fifties. In sport, a generation is ten years. When it is over you wipe the slate clean and start again. In France, the sixties had hardly begun when, one by one, Geminiani, Barbotin, Rolland and Bobet were wiped from the slate. Two years were enough to consign the photo of my *belle équipe* at the Coliseum to the souvenir album.

But the fifties generation long remained in the popular imagination. More so than any other, it seems to me. I see two factors at work here, apart from nostalgia. This generation corresponded exactly to a special era in our history: the luminous period that followed the dark years of war. We called it the Reconstruction, and it called on us to lend a hand. The French people, long deprived of hope, enthusiastically took part in the 'reconstruction effort', as they said at the time. Sport, and cycling in particular, which spanned the entire country, slotted itself neatly into this great upsurge celebrating struggle and victory.

Another happy coincidence was the simultaneous emergence of not one, but ten champions of international stature and renown. These ten men, who had experienced the war, reconstructed cycling and swept the crowds along with them as they did battle in the events that pitted each one against all the others, throughout the year. They were taken to the heart of a public that ran on flair, and filled up on enthusiasm every Sunday. It was the time when Coppi beat Bobet who beat Van Steenbergen who beat Koblet who beat Bartali who beat Ockers who beat Robic ... and it worked, because the heroes were household names, whom people were glad to call Fausto, Louison, Rik, Ugo, Gino, Stan or 'Biquet'.

It worked everywhere, all the time, because the press was running smoothly as well, and could afford to be generous with its praise. When Louison attacked, the journalists described him as 'in full dress uniform'. It was not unknown for the newspapers to have some fun – as is practically obligatory today. When I won my university championship in Budapest, in front of about 100 onlookers, the newspaper *Le Soir* invented a special correspondent named Imre Czordas, who wrote: '...A magnificent day for the French colours in Budapest. On Mount Liberty over 100,000 people met the exploits of Jean Bobet with rapturous applause...'

It worked very well.

It is not that the generations that came after the fifties were in any way inferior. Anything but. They were just different. The early 1960s saw the disappearance of the all-rounder. From Anquetil and Van Looy onwards, the stage race riders diverged from the Classic riders and, later on, the *rouleurs* from the *grimpeurs*. The all-round champions gave way to top-class specialists. It is accepted as normal that skiers, after Jean-Claude Killy, no longer win the downhill, slalom and giant slalom at the same time. It *is* normal but, every so often, an all-rounder can come along and knock the specialists off their perch. Eddy Merckx and Bernard Hinault did just that.

I am always glad to talk about Eddy Merckx. At dinner parties in town, when people who know nothing about cycling (which is their prerogative, of course), ask me to explain it to them in ten minutes (an impossible task), I enlist the help of Eddy Merckx. To demonstrate that the main story begins with the Milan–San Remo and finishes with the Tour of Lombardy, I refer constantly to him: not only did he enter more races than most, he won every type: the Classics, the Tours, the Championships. To show my erudition I also mention that, in the winter, *Six Jours* events take place on indoor tracks. It's fine: Eddy Merckx was still there, winning a fair share of those. And when the lady across the table from me, who has not quite followed the lecture, asked whether or not this Merckx won the Milan–San Remo in the end, I exult: 'Yes, Madame. He won Milan–San Remo... seven times!'

In short, Eddy Merckx is unhesitatingly, unquestionably, undisputedly THE best racing cyclist of all time. Or at least up till the present.

Louison and I talked about Merckx a great deal, on Sunday mornings. Both of us were up to our necks in thalassotherapy, a venture that was both fascinating and all-consuming. In Quiberon we were far from the peloton, but cycling was still very close to us. Monday to Saturday meant work; Sunday was for cycling.

To be more precise, on Sunday mornings we rode. The level of motivation varied from one week to the next. If I reminded Louison, 'We're riding tomorrow,' I was stating the obvious: that was the routine. If Louison called, 'Are we riding tomorrow?' it would take a little persuasion to overcome his hesitation. If, on the other hand, he addressed me with 'Tomorrow, we ride,' I knew that it would be like old times, in training. Relatively speaking, that is: I mean we might average 26kph instead of 25. Speed was no longer in our repertoire. We took pleasure elsewhere: with less violence, and more subtlety. Occasionally, we would even chance to catch a scent or a snatch of the *volupté* of yesteryear. With the wind at our backs, the intoxication was such that we almost took ourselves for the Bobet brothers. When the wind turned, we were somebody else entirely.

While riding on a Sunday morning we put the world to rights. The world as a whole, if we had had a couple of VIPs – ministers or captains of industry – in for a cure that week. Or just the world of thalassotherapy, because there was always some problem to sort out and, in the saddle, we dealt with it. But above all, we put the cycling world to rights.

In 1972 the cycling world revolved around Eddy Merckx, who beat Louison's record by winning his fourth consecutive Tour de France. Bearing no grudge, we organised a post-Tour criterium in Quiberon in August. Merckx and Poulidor (who had finished third) headed the bill for this exhibition race, consisting of 40 laps of a two-kilometre circuit on the Côte Sauvage. For logistical reasons – in August there is neither a hotel room nor a camping pitch to be found in Quiberon – Merckx stayed with Louison and Poulidor with me. The public was thrilled from the start, and went completely wild when, two laps from the finish, Merckx and Poulidor broke away from the peloton. In the grandstand Louison whispered that 'twenty years later, these two can put on just as good a show as we did.'

Meanwhile, the two escapees were also sharing a secret or two. Poulidor suggested to Merckx that he would like to win, in order to offer the flowers to Madame Bobet.' His opponent, pedalling harder, retorted: 'Me, too.' At the finishing line it was Merckx first, Poulidor second. Merckx grabbed the bouquet and Poulidor offered his excuses to Mme. Bobet.

It was enough to make you want to write a fable about the strong man and the kind man.

Riding on a Sunday morning we had plenty of ideas: some bright ones, some not so good, and even some that were completely mad. It was not long before the Landes de Lanvaux (altitude 147m, in the north of the Département of Morbihan) had us dreaming of the Izoard and the Galibier. Fully aware of the difficulty of such an enterprise, we increased the length of our Sunday bike rides in order to clock up the bare minimum of 3,000 kilometres by the end of June. In 1974 we attacked via the Galibier. We invited Pierrot Barbotin and Raymond Le Bert (the quarrel of 1958 long forgotten) along for the ride: Grenoble–Galibier, 150 kilometres, by way of the Col du Glandon and the Col de la Croix-de-Fer.

We could certainly have done with better weather. From the very start, the rain forced us to put on the hated rain capes, and in Vizille, at 20 kilometres, we were seriously asking ourselves whether all this was really such a good idea. In the Romanche Valley we were so thoroughly sprayed by the lorries that we were soaked to the bone when we reached the bottom of the first col. Raymond Le Bert, in his car, kept handing out hot drinks (this was in July) and assuring us that 'It's nothing, my lads, the weather's about to improve.' Raymond was right: the weather did improve at 1,000m, but our rain-stiffened legs did not. On the ascent of the Croix-de-Fer we were literally steaming, as our bodies warmed up and dried the wet clothes. It made us laugh. We were still laughing in the Maurienne Valley, where the wind was favourable. We were not laughing quite so much on the Col du Télégraphe, in spite of the magnificent view. We were not laughing at all when we left Valloire. The morning's bad weather had significantly reduced our average speed and we were running about an hour behind schedule. At the same time, as we passed 1,500m, it turned cold and we were feeling pretty hollow. We had another ten kilometres to climb – no point quibbling: we were at Plan-Lachat and knew the area – and all three of us suddenly felt ravenous. We began to zig-zag across the road, making more lateral than forward progress. An appalled Raymond told us to 'keep playing nicely, little ones,' and that he would 'be off to sort something out'.

We found him in the middle of the road two kilometres further up, gesticulating wildly. We eventually hauled ourselves up to him. He pushed our shattered frames through the door of the last farm chalet of the village. Inside we found a fire blazing in the hearth and, on the table, three plates of omelette cooked in rum. Or perhaps it was rum cooked in omelette, I do not remember exactly. We were able to laugh again when our hostess, overcome at the sight of Louison Bobet in her house, from which she had seen so many Tours de France go by, said to him: 'Oh, Monsieur Bobet, this is the first time you have dropped in!' It was nearly dark and a storm was threatening when we took our leave. We climbed the last five kilometres of the Galibier in no time at all. Dismounting at the summit, 2,400 metres above the Landes de Lanvaux, we hugged Raymond, and he embraced us. And I said to myself that this man, with or without his magic bottle, could still work miracles.

In 1975 we decided to indulge in the ultimate luxury: the Izoard. We prepared our stage assiduously: one hundred and fifty kilometres from Embrun to Briançon, via the Ubaye Valley, the col de Vars, the Guil Valley, the Casse Déserte and the Col de l'Izoard. This time we chose the right day for it: the weather was glorious.

At the age of 50 Louison approached the adventure as a pilgrimage to his favourite hunting ground, his private domain of the fifties. The only problem was that, even if Louison was in his own backyard, he was not in very good shape. From the very first kilometres I sensed that he was out of breath. It was really bad luck, and soon became a nightmare. We were supposed to be enjoying ourselves and even, perhaps, 'having a little go, to remind our legs what it feels like'. Instead, Louison was glued to my back wheel, his lips pressed tightly together. Kilometre after kilometre I feared it was his toe-clips that would be first to open, and he would abandon the whole thing. After Barcelonnette the road began to go gently uphill. Still not a word. At the real beginning of the Col de Vars I realised what was in store for me. It was going to be the tow up the Col d'Abetone from the 1953 Giro, all over again. It was the perfect rerun. I gave him a drink and did everything not to get more than a metre ahead. He followed. With some alarm, because we were only just half-way, I wondered what on earth we were going to do. But everything comes eventually, and so did the top of the Vars. The white line marking the summit never fades from one year to the next. As soon as I spotted it I slowed down imperceptibly to leave the way clear. As the lead climber, I thought it might be a polite gesture.

The plunge down to Guillestre was much more fun. My client enjoyed himself cutting the corners, and I enjoyed following him at last. In the Guil Valley, as long as a day without bread, disillusionment set in. Immured in his silence Louison took refuge in my rear wheel once more. I had plenty of time to work out that we could carry on like this for another three hours at the most. At the sign for 'Arvieux, 4km', the zombie on my back drew level because 'He wouldn't mind a drink from the fountain: you know, in front of the church.' He stayed beside me, took off his sunglasses and painstakingly wiped his face. At the fountain, we did not stop. Just enough time to fill two bottles. And off we went again. Or rather, off he went. And I followed.

The hard part of the Izoard comes when you leave Arvieux, up to the hamlet of Brunissart, before you reach the forest. It is a treacherous, insidious 11 per-cent, because you cannot see the damned slope amongst the last, vast pastures. I felt it though, especially when the zombie from a few minutes before started pressing down on his pedals, the hypocrite. I started breathing a little more heavily, and immediately wished I hadn't. I am sure that, at that moment, Louison heard the last sighs of Kubler and Wagtmans as he dropped them. And the bastard dropped me! Five metres, ten metres, then 50, and my fine Louison ascended into his kingdom. Without a backward glance. In the Casse Déserte he left me 200 metres behind, but that suited me because it allowed me another sight of the Louison of 1953, when Coppi furtively saluted him a month after the Albetone. I really had seen everything, then, in a single day. At the summit of the Izoard he was waiting for me – ten metres beyond the white line, which he had crossed first. On the descent towards Briançon it struck me that Merckx and Bobet were two of a kind.

On Sunday mornings, then, we rode for our own great pleasure. Until one day in 1976, when Louison pulled a new Loreto on me.

I will attempt to describe a long and painful business in just a few lines. Louison had recently sold the majority of his shares in his Thalassotherapy Institute to a large commercial bank. This arrangement in no way affected my work as its General Director. The bank left me at the reins, and I felt quite comfortable with the arrangement. It was Louison who lost his way. He was still President, but no longer the proprietor. He could not accept this because, it is true to say, he really was the one who had invented and built it all. When a certain Jacques Borel, then the reviled king of Restoroute motorway services, entered the bank's boardroom his sole obsession was to get rid of Louison, whose charisma he could not stand. He cooked up a diabolical scheme and Louison fell into the trap. In full dress uniform, I am tempted to say. Within two minutes of an extraordinarily brief board meeting, he was dismissed, sent packing. My own resignation letter, which I had slipped into his pocket as a last resort, did not change a thing.

It was Loreto all over again. Except that this time Louison was thrown completely off-balance, lost his head and became angry with me for being cast into the street because of him. After a few weeks I was engaged by a different group of financiers to oversee the construction and launch of a new thalassotherapy centre at Carnac. And Louison was still not talking to me.

On Sunday mornings I rode. Alone, of course. Then one day, on a minor road among the Carnac menhirs, it happened, as it was bound to sooner or later. Along came Louison in the other direction. The twain were going to meet. I picked him out at 100 metres, glanced up at 20, and then stopped looking. So did he, as far as I could tell. Two minutes later I heard the squeal of a tyre behind me. It was Louison. He had turned round. He came alongside and, in a tone that did not really sound like either forgiveness or an apology, he said: 'Ok, that'll do. Tomorrow, we ride.'

We took that ride in the Basque country.

From 1979 we were engaged in another fascinating and time-consuming venture, and a kind of revenge match: the Biarritz Thalassotherapy Institute.

On Sunday mornings we enjoyed ourselves on the roads which follow the River Nive upstream, as far as Saint-Jean-Pied-de-Port or Saint-Étienne-de-Baïgorry. The interior of the Basque country was so beautiful that there was no need to ask, on a Saturday evening, whether we would ride tomorrow. When I wanted to increase the distance, however, for example by climbing up to the Iraty Forest, Louison began to grumble and let me go on my own. He always found an excuse not to come. I was not fooled. He was tired, tired all the time. So I concocted some shorter excursions to distract him and take him away from bad company. Louison was in and out of hospital, seeing lots of surgeons. We would not ride tomorrow, we would just roll along the flat banks of the Adour. Not too far, not too fast. We forced ourselves to believe that better days would come. After all, we were both in a position to know that, in cycling, you sometimes come back from this far off.

XIII

CHIBERTA

After he became ill – with that filthy tumour, which they confirmed to me as incurable – Louison ceased to be Louison.

As a child, as a teenager, as a champion – especially as a champion – Louison used to complain a lot. If he hurt himself, say, or was worried about something. Our mother was in the habit of saying that her Louison upset himself too much. Geminiani used to say, jokingly, that Louison needed to complain in order to bounce back.

Louison was not complaining any more.

However, I knew that he was suffering: to some extent physically, but a good deal more psychologically. When he came down to my office (his flat was above the Thalassotherapy Institute), he kept a close watch on himself. Sometimes, he let it slip that the night had not been... then he caught himself and broke off. His nights concerned nobody but himself. I did not press him, not knowing in which direction to take the conversation. I was stupid, useless. Then I cheated, by feigning false excitement. I announced astronomical reservation figures and full bookings, inflated by 20 per-cent. His face lit up. He made me go over these promising prospects again, drawing my attention, as usual, to the pessimism of my provisional budget. And then, every time, he added that I was really lucky to have so much work. What was I to reply without saying something clumsy that would hurt him, or something artificial that would hurt him even more? I felt useless and stupid.

One day he arrived in a determined and voluble mood. Out of the blue he suggested that we should go for a ride. Go out for a ride together, as in the good old days. I was not surprised. I had the impression that the same idea had occurred to me at exactly the same moment. I was convinced that nothing could bring him more pleasure than going for a ride. And I was just as sure that I would be able to keep him going straight if we pedalled shoulder to shoulder, to counter the imbalance that pulled him irresistibly to the right.

Tomorrow, we would ride...

The preparations were painstaking. I searched out a two-kilometre circuit in the most sheltered and most tucked-away corner of the Parc de Chiberta, in Anglet. Caution was of the essence: I knew that the *paparazzi* would be looking out for him on the promenade of the beach at Biarritz. There were three of us surrounding him to help him out of his car and into the saddle. He let himself be carried. But, as soon as we were on our bikes, he was in command. He chose the gear ratio – his, and therefore mine as well – to cruise smoothly at twenty-five kilometres an hour. He managed to get away at the first attempt. He was holding himself more stiffly, gripping his handlebars harder, but it was the old Louison.

Almost the same as before. He was pressing ever more heavily on my left shoulder, and asked me if everything was all right; I heard him mutter 'Great, great.' We completed the circuit. He decided to do another one. I had a terrifying vision of falling and bringing him down with me. In a sort of euphoria we rode faster and faster until he suddenly cried, 'Let me go!' I did nothing of the kind. 'Let me go!' he cried again. I slowed down and moved aside. I let go. He veered off to the right and collapsed onto a fortuitously placed patch of grass. I rushed over to him. He was unhurt. But the look in his eyes… A distraught expression, a look that said that all was lost. Completely.

Louison stopped coming down to my office for a chat. He knew that I knew why. He did not want to show anyone his body, propped up by two walking sticks, his face disfigured by cortisone. One Sunday morning it was his wife, Françoise, who came to see me. Françoise was showing great courage in the face of the storm, but that morning she was all at sea. Her efforts, and mine, to dissuade Louison from going to vote the following day were in vain. He could not go a single step without assistance. We kept telling him that it was not a sensible idea, or even a feasible one. He would not hear a word of it. Having run out of arguments I suggested taking him to the polling station in one of the Institute's wheelchairs, convinced that he would refuse to appear in public so diminished, so disabled. An invalid. To my utter amazement, he agreed. At the polling station, on the Sunday morning, he slipped his ballot paper into the box, looked hard into the eyes of the Mayor of Biarritz, and pronounced in a strong voice, 'Vote cast.'

The following Sunday, he escaped.

For a long time afterwards I went riding with his shadow. All over: in Brittany, in the Basque Country. But never so well as on the Izoard.

191